scrapped
PRINCeSS
a taLe of DestINY

Story by
ICHIRO SAKAKI

Illustrated by
YUKINOBU AZUMI

POP
FICTION

STORY	Ichiro Sakaki
ILLUSTRATIONS	Yukinobu Azumi
TRANSLATION	Paul Kotta
ENGLISH ADAPTATION	Lianne Sentar
DESIGN AND LAYOUT	James Lee
	and Jose Macasocol, Jr.
COVER DESIGN	Al-Insan Lashley
ART DIRECTOR	Anne Marie Horne
SENIOR EDITOR	Nicole Monastirsky
JUNIOR EDITOR	Kara Stambach
DIGITAL IMAGING MANAGER	Chris Buford
PRODUCTION MANAGER	Elisabeth Brizzi
MANAGING EDITOR	Vy Nguyen
EDITOR-IN-CHIEF	Rob Tokar
VP OF PRODUCTION	Ron Klamert
PRESIDENT AND C.O.O.	John Parker
PUBLISHER	Mike Kiley
C.E.O. & CHIEF CREATIVE OFFICER	Stuart Levy

First TOKYOPOP printing: October 2006

10 9 8 7 6 5 4 3 2 1

Printed in the USA

SCRAPPED PRINCESS
SUTENEKO OUJYO NO ZENSOUKYOKU
© ICHIRO SAKAKI, YUKINOBU AZUMI 1999.
First published in Japan in 1999 by
KADOKAWA SHOTEN PUBLISHING CO., LTD., Tokyo.
English translation rights arranged with
KADOKAWA SHOTEN PUBLISHING CO., LTD., Tokyo
through TUTTLE–MORI AGENCY, INC., Tokyo.

English text copyright © 2006 TOKYOPOP Inc.

Library of Congress Cataloging-in-Publication Data
Sakaki, Ichiro, 1969-
   [Sukurappudo purinsesu. English]
   Scrapped princess : a tale of destiny / story by Ichiro
Sakaki ; illustrated by Yukinobu Azumi ; [translation, Paul
Kotta ; English adaptation, Lianne Sentar].

    p.   cm.
Audience: 13-17.
   ISBN 1-59532-984-6 (v. 1)
   I. Azumi, Yukinobu. II. Kotta, Paul. III. Sentar, Lianne.
IV. Title.
PZ49.31.S36413 2006   2006010396
[Fic]--dc22

contents

PROLOGUE

Five simultaneous screams ripped through the cathedral. They echoed through the halls for a moment, resounding the stone walls, before finally tapering into an oppressive silence.

The crowd, frozen in place, cast its collective gaze on the five white doors that sealed off five identical rooms. Since it was impossible to know what had taken place behind those doors, or why it had happened in all five rooms at the same time, the crowd could only stand in fear and wait.

After a moment, a dark red liquid began to ooze from the cracks at the bottom of the doorways. There was so much of it that the crowd didn't realize what it was at first—blood, thick and glistening, dark and bountiful.

The doors opened in silent unison. On the floor of each narrow chamber lay a man soaked in red. Thick blood flowed from the men's mouths, ears, eyes, and pores; deep crimson plumes bloomed against the pure white of their robes.

The men should have been dead, and yet they still breathed. Their limbs began to twitch, barely at first, before slowly dragging their bodies across the floor. They writhed like slugs, leaving long, red trails in their wake.

The five stopped simultaneously and opened their mouths. They coughed, dripping scarlet down their lips, as the lids over their blood-blinded eyes quivered.

"Listen well!" they called. "All of you . . . we have heard the prophecy!"

The onlookers stirred in anxious panic.

"In the name of the all-powerful god Mauser, we have heard the 5111th Oracle of Saint Grendel and we convey it to you!"

A prophecy—the infallible word of the divine, a celestial insight into the future no mortal could ever duplicate. It was precisely what those gathered in the cathedral had waited so long to hear.

"The infant girl must be . . ."

The five martyrs' eyes rolled back as they chanted their message, their words filling the crowd with shock, then confusion, then, as the full weight of the message became clear, fear.

It was the year 5111 of the Continental Calendar, six months after the royal family of the Kingdom of Linevan had officially sealed the Mauser Church, and the 5111th Oracle of Saint Grendel had at last concluded.

⚬❦⚬

A young girl silently picked her way through the darkened woods, the moonlight that spilled through the foliage barely lighting her way. She kept a steady pace, holding her breath, her face anxious. The fear of accidentally tripping in the dark was all that kept her from breaking into a run.

The girl carried a bundle—something wrapped in a soft cloth. She held it with great care, but her hands gripped the fabric so tightly that her fingers turned white.

A clearing finally loomed ahead.

The girl stepped out of the brush and hurried over to the edge of a small spring, the moon reflecting on its surface dimly illuminating her surroundings.

"Mistress Carol," she breathed as if in prayer, her amber eyes darting back and forth. Upon finding the clearing empty save for her, the anxiety on her young face grew even more intense.

"Mistress Carol!" she chanted, almost as if to calm herself. "Mistress Carol, Mistress Car—"

A hand clapped over her mouth from behind.

Just as she was about to erupt into a panic, a low, assuring voice murmured, "Easy."

The air in front of the girl rippled. The distortion faded in and out before widening—like a painting sliced open with a knife—to reveal a petite young woman. She had braided silver hair; a long navy outfit draped over her slight curves.

The woman appeared to be in her mid-twenties, and had the kind of dignified, intelligent poise that disconcerted others. She focused her ruby-red eyes on the girl.

The hand over the girl's mouth retracted. "Mistress Carol," the girl sighed in relief. She turned and looked over her shoulder.

A large man stood behind her, wrapped in hardened leather armor. He wore a single-edged sword known as a *tachi* on his waist. He looked about thirty-five years old, with black hair, black eyes, and a face somehow foreign. A hint of savageness lurked in his features, though his eyes gleamed with pleasant mischief. He smiled disarmingly.

The girl's grip on her bundle relaxed. "Master Yuma," she mumbled.

"I'm sorry, Claire," Carol said calmly as she stepped over to the girl. "Did we frighten you?"

"A b-bit," Claire replied, her heart pounding in her chest.

Carol stroked Claire's hair before carefully taking the bundle from the girl's arms. Peering inside the folds, Carol smiled. "Aw."

Yuma crouched down for a look. "Wow," he agreed. "It *is* cute. What's its name?"

Claire swallowed and answered solemnly, "She doesn't have one."

Yuma sighed and looked back toward the forest. The moon peeked out from beyond the treetops, revealing the outline of a massive structure that loomed imposingly

over the landscape. The forest itself was but a small section of the structure's sprawling grounds.

"Let us handle this," Carol told the girl before she and Yuma took their leave. Claire called out to them hesitantly. Only Yuma turned around; Carol looked steadfastly ahead, as if to shield herself against anything the girl could say.

"I-I have a message for you b-both," Claire explained. She swallowed, then recited, " 'We're counting on you.' "

Yuma nodded. The girl bowed deeply before spinning on her heels. Yuma shifted his gaze from her retreating form to look at Carol, then sighed again.

"Give her a break, will you?"

"No," Carol said through a clenched jaw. "I never would've guessed she could be so cold-hearted." Her voice held the bitterness of one betrayed.

"Think of her position—don't judge her like she's one of the others. After all, she risked her life to get the baby here. Isn't that proof she loves it?"

"If I . . ." Carol bit her tongue, swallowed, then tried again. "If I learned that Shannon and Raquel were to be killed, I'd throw away the world to protect them."

"Not everyone's as strong as you," Yuma said quietly.

"No one's truly strong, Yuma. I'm not, you're not—people are *weak*. But that's exactly why we have to . . . to . . ." She trailed off, sobbing softly.

Yuma put his arm around her as they began to walk again. She sniffed, pressed her cheek against his shoulder, and allowed herself to be led along.

"We should give her a name," she said at last.

"I guess." As he voiced his agreement, Yuma furrowed his brow.

"Something everyone will like."

"Sure. I'm just . . . not sure which names are normal, and which ones will make your children hate you." His voice, tinged with a hint of a foreign accent, emphasized his point.

Carol shot him a look. "Come to think of it, you laughed when you first heard *my* name, my dear."

"I already told you that was instinctual," he protested. "I didn't mean anything by it. Besides—you said my name was weird when you first heard it."

"*I* was just a kid."

"Right," Yuma muttered, turning away. "And I'm just some dirty, old scoundrel who teases girls ten years his junior."

She chuckled at his pout. "I think we're both scoundrels this time. We're kidnappers, maybe even . . ." She smiled bitterly and shrugged. Even *she* wasn't sure how many laws they were breaking.

"Anyway, there's no hurry on the name. Her life's just beginning." Carol smiled at the sleeping infant.

Yuma waved a hand dismissively. "As long as you don't leave it up to me," he said, "take as long as you want."

The couple walked onward, their sure steps conveying their resolve to disregard the obstacles in their way—status, honor, their past, common sense—and their desire to ignore everyone who might remind them of that.

the end of the days of innocence

The blazing orange globe of the sun barely peeked over the horizon. A young woman, still in bed, let out a lazy groan and blinked open her sky-blue eyes.

"Nn."

Unlike her older brother and sister—both with low blood pressure—she didn't require a wake-up call in the morning. Instead, she jumped out of bed to shake the sleepiness out of her, plopped down on the stool in front of her sister's hand-me-down vanity, and snatched up a comb. Still yawning, she brushed out her long blonde hair and started braiding it in a careful, practiced manner.

The girl was in her early teens, with a pretty face and a developing but graceful figure. Although there was something endearing and almost kitten-esque about her appearance, her mannerisms suggested a catlike daring and slyness. Everyone had seemingly contradictory qualities; in her case, the contradictions appeared just a little sharper. Almost to prove this point, she daintily stroked her braids, then changed from her nightgown into brown work-clothes that looked about as feminine as an anvil.

She smiled at herself in the mirror and slapped both palms against her cheeks. "Right!" she cried, dropping to the floor. She began some sort of bizarre stretching routine in a slow awkward manner, like someone imitating a dance they'd seen. She continued until she cried out in pain and grabbed her cramped leg.

Hobbling slightly as she got to her feet, she puffed up her cheeks and exhaled sharply. She curled up one side of her mouth (to her it was a tough-looking grin) and sneered, "Desert Eagle, say your prayers."

And with that, Pacifica Casull, the youngest daughter in the Casull family, strode out of her room.

༺♦༻

The walled city of Manurhin hemmed the western frontier of the Linevan Kingdom, a monarchal nation in the Dustbin Continent. While Manurhin was officially considered a city, in reality it was little more than a small country town with a barricade and a man named Luigis Franki serving as the duke of the city.

Thanks to the benevolent rule of Duke Franki, living standards in Manurhin were high (despite the backwater nature of the city), but Manurhin was best known as a stopover spot for self-proclaimed adventurers—rogues and scoundrels hoping to strike it rich in the vast expanse of unexplored territory beyond the city. Manurhin had the same sorts of things found everywhere, but, unbeknownst to most, it *did* have something unique.

At the far edge of Manurhin's commercial district stood a simple two-story brick building, uncommon for a city where exceptionally cheap land had pushed multiple-story homes out of style. The building, labeled with a crudely chiseled sign that read: *Casull Weapons Shop*, served as store, warehouse, and home to Yuma Casull and his three children. Behind the building lay a huge yard, complete with garden and small pond; Yuma Casull believed in self-sufficiency, and thus grew vegetables in his garden, raised fish in his pond, and had a dozen or so chickens running around in his yard.

As the early morning sun bathed the town in its soft light, a young man looked around the store and sleepily scratched his head. His handsome face, featuring an elegantly shaped nose, was offset by a constant, grumpy squint that hid his black eyes. That and his stooped posture combined to create a world-weary look that somehow suited him more than the youthful vibrancy normally expected of a twenty-year-old. Straightening the collar of his nightshirt, he walked through the dimly lit shop.

"Pacifica!" he called, brushing hair off his shoulder. His long, disheveled mane had been hastily tied into a ponytail. "Hey, Pacifica!"

The room the young man searched contained a wide variety of merchandise in addition to the advertised weapons: hunting gear, carpentry tools, household goods, and a rack of vegetables stocked by the family's personal garden. Above the vegetables hung a message board used by adventurers. It bore notes ranging from the generic "Companion Wanted!" to the somewhat shady "Treasure Map for Sale!" (Either because of the owner's broad interests or simple good policy, the store sold any merchandise that would fit through its doors.)

The vegetables on display, however, had all wilted, and the most recent message on the board was more than ten days old. The stale air inside the store suggested that the place hadn't been open for business in several days.

"Pacifica!" the young man shouted again, to no reply. He was Shannon Casull, eldest son of the Casull family, and he made no attempt to hide his annoyance. Changing his strategy, he began looking in closets and under counters.

"Where are you?" he murmured as he peered into some boxes. He tentatively opened a drawer.

"I don't see how she could be hiding in there," came a voice from the back of the store. "Maybe she's in the garden?"

Shannon glanced up. His older sister, Raquel, descended the stairs in a pink nightgown.

She resembled Shannon in looks and general physique, but she emanated a youthful and infectious happiness. Her nightgown had an embroidered cat on one lapel, and she wore a nightcap with a furry white ball on top—uncommon attire for someone her age, but

it somehow suited her. Her pretty features were soft and relaxed, and unlike Shannon, her calm wasn't restricted to the short moments after waking up in the morning.

"In the garden?" Shannon repeated. "This early?"

"The matches. You know."

"She's been fighting with Desert Eagle?"

The two paused to yawn. Neither of them was a morning person.

Shannon rubbed his eyes. "She never *learns*," he snapped as he swept past Raquel. "Fine. I'll go get her."

Raquel gave a floppy wave. "Be careful," she warned halfheartedly as he disappeared out the back door.

❧

All living things fought for survival. Every creature took life; it was an unavoidable sin. A struggle simply for power, rather than survival, might have been ultimately meaningless, but only a fool who didn't see the world as it truly was sought to avoid *all* battles. The strong lived on—to be alive was to already be at war.

Now my brain's ready, Pacifica thought as she spread her feet. *Time for battle.*

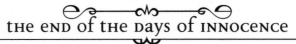

Pacifica's father had taught her the art of mentally preparing for combat. As she summoned her courage for the fight, she bent her legs and balled her fists under her chin.

The girl was nearly equal in ability to her opponent, but she'd suffered the humiliation of seven consecutive defeats due to her impatient and unsuccessful first strikes. She knew that the battle wouldn't last more than an instant—it never did—and that whoever struck first would lose. The enemy, perhaps sensing the intensity of Pacifica's fighting spirit, made no unnecessary movement and merely fixed cold eyes on her.

Just then, Shannon's sleepy voice rang through the yard. "Pacifica!"

His voice shattered the tension. Pacifica attacked.

"Aaaiiiyaaaa!"

"Grrraawwww!

Pacifica explosively launched her secret attack technique: the Killer Hurricane Special Number Two. (She'd come up with the name herself, but hadn't yet decided what it meant.) The enemy responded with a brutal jumping kick, also meant to end the brawl immediately. The combatants collided with a violent impact.

For an instant, the two warriors stood back to back, frozen in the last stances of their respective attacks . . . and then Pacifica made a low, pained groan and fell over with a thud. She writhed on the ground, a distinct red mark on her cheek branding her with defeat.

"I lost *again,*" she moaned.

"Good effort," her brother offered as he looked down at her. Pacifica responded with a malevolent glare.

"A defeated warrior needs no praise!" she snapped.

"You should take any praise you can get." Shannon raised his eyes from the crawling Pacifica to the creature that had defeated her. "You must be the only person in the world who would risk life and limb for an omelet."

Desert Eagle clucked contemptuously. The brute of a chicken was no ordinary fowl. Desert Eagle was notorious throughout the neighborhood for stopping short only at murder to protect her eggs. She'd permanently traumatized a number of trespassing animals.

Tears of frustration welled up in Pacifica's eyes. "But Desert Eagle's eggs are the *best!*" she complained. "They give me the strength of ten men!"

"But are they worth dying for?" Shannon watched the hen strut back to her eggs with an almost regal air.

Pacifica clenched her fists and glared at the winter sky. "I'll show that bird who's boss tomorrow," she vowed. "Just watch me—I'll do it!"

"Right." Shannon bent over to give his sister a hand up. "Just call it quits for today, would you? I need some help."

Pacifica took the offered hand. "Help?" she repeated meekly. She knew what he needed, but she'd been dreading it for days.

Shannon sighed. "Yeah," he said quietly. "I can't do the funeral by myself."

❦

A crowd of townspeople watched as flames slowly engulfed the wooden coffin. The cremation was all there was to the funeral—no ceremony, no priest reciting prayers, nothing religious in the slightest. The fire reached farther and farther skyward, scattering sparks into the atmosphere before eventually fading. Perhaps comparing the flames to the transient nature of life was overly sentimental, but such were Shannon's thoughts as he silently watched his father's body turn to ash.

The simplicity of it all had been Yuma Casull's wish. In the Linevan Kingdom, a funeral normally included ceremonies prescribed by the official Mauser faith. But Shannon's father had wanted no such thing, for some reason.

His eyes fixed on the embers, Shannon called out softly to Pacifica. "Hey."

"What?" she replied as she rubbed her nose along her sleeve. Her mourning clothes didn't fit her very well.

"It's . . . it's okay to cry."

"Father said he didn't want anything depressing at his funeral," she murmured. "Don't worry about me." *Besides*, she almost added. *I've already cried enough.* She and Shannon both knew that.

"It's weird, though," she admitted quietly. "I feel . . . different from how I thought I would."

The last of the coffin and its contents dissipated into dust and smoke, giving the funeral a simple and quiet ending, typical of Yuma's native land. The crowd began to disperse.

Judging from the turnout, Yuma Casull had been widely loved and respected—neighbors, friends, and even adventurers and peddlers passing through had gathered in the town square for his cremation. Yuma's children were surprised at the large number in attendance, but one guest in particular was most unexpected.

"Is that the duke?" asked a voice in the crowd.

Shannon turned to see a figure at the edge of the square. It was a man around fifty years of age, with a stern, dignified face and quiet eyes. He was dressed in black mourning clothes similar to those worn by everyone else, but even the simplicity of his garb couldn't hide his stateliness and elegance. A black-clothed woman stood in silent attendance beside him.

Shannon knew the man from official events in town: Luigis Franki, Duke of Manurhin. Shannon found himself wondering what "difficulties" of the aristocratic lifestyle had given the duke his worry lines. Like his father, Shannon had an irreverent attitude toward people of status.

Shannon and Raquel glanced at each other. They knew the duke's reputation for being a kind and benevolent ruler, but why would a nobleman personally attend the funeral of a commoner?

Duke Franki slowly walked over to the Casull siblings and a very confused-looking Pacifica. Even she knew that an aristocrat venturing outdoors normally brought several imposing bodyguards, but the small woman with the duke didn't look like a bodyguard at all. Her age was difficult to guess, but she seemed to be in her mid-twenties, with flaxen hair, cut short as a young boy's, and cold detachment written across her sharp features.

Shannon noticed that her upper body didn't move much when she walked, which meant one thing: she knew how to fight.

"You are the family of Yuma Casull?" the woman asked with crisp politeness. Her mouth smiled, but her gray eyes did not. "As I'm sure you know, this is the duke of Manurhin, His Grace Luigis Franki."

The three siblings dropped to one knee in deference. The duke waved them up and smiled, the sternness in his face suddenly melting away.

"Let's omit the formalities, my dear," he told his attendant. "I'm here unannounced. I knew your father personally," the duke explained, his voice quieting. "I've come to pay my respects—not as Duke, but as an acquaintance."

Pacifica's eyes widened. *Father knew the duke?*

"Thank you, Your Grace," Shannon replied evenly.

Neither his words nor his tone betrayed his inner trepidation. "I'm sure Father would have been pleased."

"Yes." The duke cleared his throat, then went on in a friendly but careful tone. "And, ah, what are your plans at this point?"

"Plans?" Shannon glanced at his sisters. "We haven't talked about that yet, but I suppose I'll take over Father's store."

"I see." The duke lowered his gaze. When he looked back up at the siblings, he spoke rather abruptly. "And did your father leave a will?"

Shannon's eyebrows furrowed. "Well . . . Father died suddenly, in an accident." Shannon had been told so by the City Guard; he hadn't actually seen his father die.

"Of course, but your father was a man who planned ahead. Widower that he was, I assume he left some sort of written instructions for his children in the event of some misfortune."

The siblings looked confused, so the duke quickly held out his hands. "Although it's none of my business," he added. "I just thought that perhaps he . . . left a message for me."

The black-clad attendant inserted herself between the duke and the siblings, cutting off the conservation.

"Your Grace," she said briskly. "You must be going. Important duties await."

The duke let out a breath. "Is it that late already?" he murmured. "Well, then, I must take my leave."

The duke turned on his heels and walked smartly away, his attendant in perfect lockstep. Shannon almost called after them, but decided against it.

The man was a duke; no matter how puzzled, Shannon was in no position to question Duke Franki's curiosity.

Pacifica voiced her siblings' silent concerns. "Weird," she muttered. "What was that all about?"

❧

As the old expression went: "A crowd is the best place to hide." A heavy, middle-aged man proved the cliché to be true as he stood among the mourners, his tongue darting in and out to moisten his reptilian-like lips.

"Is that the duke?" he grunted.

Wesson, the local carpenter, stood directly in front of the man. He turned to face him. "Excuse me?"

"The duke." The man pointed. "Look."

Wesson's gaze followed the stout finger. "That's him," he agreed, returning his eyes to the stranger. Foreigners and passing adventurers weren't unusual in Manurhin, so the fact that the heavy man wasn't a local—or that he had slicked reddish hair, oily skin, and dirty clothes—didn't draw much attention.

"And who would've thought?" Wesson commented. "The duke himself, coming to Yuma Casull's funeral."

"Was Mister Casull an important man?"

"No, he just owned a small weapons shop. The adventurers took a liking to him." Wesson paused. "On the other hand," he added, "Yuma never talked about what he did before he came to town. And he *was* an odd one, not unlike how the duke is a bit eccentric. Maybe that's why they got along."

"That so?" The stranger nodded intently, like an investigator taking down new information.

"Sure. Any particular reason you're asking about Yuma?"

"We had some dealings together once," the stranger said with a shrug. "I'm just, y'know . . . curious."

The man excused himself from Wesson and squeezed his way out of the throng of mourners. When he was far enough away from the mob, his thin, wet lips distorted into a sly grin.

"Interesting," he murmured. "Maybe I should pay a visit to the good duke."

Someone who wanted to lose himself in a crowd was often deceptive or troubled. Or, in those rare cases . . . were planning a professional murder.

"Getting rid of the girl will be child's play," the man said to himself, snickering at his own pun. "But I've lost seven men already. I think the deal needs a little sweetening."

The rotund man wrapped his drab olive cloak more tightly around his girth as he exited the city square. "I wonder," he mused under his breath. "What's Sinner up to today?"

⁊⁊

A slightly off-key note sprung from the plucked string, reverberating softly in the still, quiet room before fading into silence.

Shannon frowned. "That didn't sound good," he murmured as he reassessed his lute. He took a tuning fork from the case and tapped it against his leg, then started tightening and adjusting the strings.

Shannon knew that he had more important things to do than play his old lute, but with the funeral over, he felt like taking some time for himself for a change. His sisters had set out to go through their father's old belongings; never very good at organizing things, Shannon had retreated to keep from getting in the way. Besides, the chore made Shannon uncomfortable—he felt that clearing out his father's possessions was like trying to rid the house of every trace of the man's existence.

"I guess women are more practical," he mumbled to himself.

Alone in his sparse room (contrary to Raquel's chambers, which were bursting with books and knick-knacks), Shannon realized, not for the first time, that the place could even strike *him* as unwelcoming. He also realized how long it had been since he'd last played his lute.

When his mother had first taught him the instrument, he'd become absorbed in singing and playing music and had even considered performing. A scowl crossed his face as he thought of how unadventurous he'd become.

Of course, for the past several years, his father's rigorous fencing lessons had left Shannon little time for any other pursuits.

It wasn't that Shannon disliked fencing, but his father's obsession with swordsmanship had always been puzzling. Yuma had never volunteered any kind of explanation.

And now I can't ask him anymore, Shannon thought.

A knock came at the door. "I'm coming in," said a soft voice.

Shannon looked up. Raquel entered the room, her sleeves rolled up and her long, black hair in a ponytail. She was definitely in organization-mode.

"I found something," Raquel explained as she drew an envelope from her pocket. It was a plain envelope with a broken seal, but Shannon could immediately guess its contents.

"Father's will?" he asked flatly.

"Mm." Raquel handed the letter to her brother. With furrowed eyebrows, Shannon slid the letter out of its confines. It *had* to be a will . . . but why had a man in the prime of his life written such a thing?

Was he expecting to die suddenly?

"Duke Franki was right," Shannon murmured, recalling the duke's nervous curiosity. "And you noticed the wound on Father's back?"

Raquel nodded. "It was from a knife. There's no doubt in my mind."

It had been the sort of small wound that a less observant person could miss, but not the Casull siblings. Their father had drilled Shannon in martial arts and Raquel in dagger self-defense; the training had included how to treat blade injuries. Both of them recognized the type of wound they'd found on their father's lower back.

Yuma's dead body had been discovered by the City Guard. In most small towns, a citizen's patrol kept the peace, but Manurhin had its own City Guard despite its small population.

The unit of professional protectors reported only to Duke Franki—in other words, the duke was in a perfect position to suppress any clues the guards had discovered about Yuma's death.

"Some accident," Shannon growled. "That bastard is hiding something."

Shannon unfolded the letter, crammed with his father's familiar handwriting. He began to read aloud:

My dear Raquel and Shannon,
Now that I've died, I have an important mission for the two of you.

Shannon looked up at his sister. "Important mission?" he repeated.

Your mother and I gave you life for this very day. You know, I took your mother in my arms, one thing led to the next, and pretty soon your mother was saying, 'Oh, stop! No, you brute, no! Oh, my, what's that feeling? Oh, oh, YES! DON'T STOP!' You know.

Shannon groaned and slumped over the table.

"Father was always joking around," Raquel said with a sniff, wiping at her moist eyes.

"Hilarious." Shannon continued to read. As his gaze moved over the handwritten lines, his eyebrows began to rise.

Fourteen years earlier, Yuma Nambu Casull and his wife Carol Casull had been asked by "a friend" to take care of an infant that they named Pacifica. Shannon and

Raquel already knew that part of the story, as did Pacifica herself; although they'd been young at the time, Shannon and his sister could remember the day their mother and father had brought the swaddled newborn home.

What Shannon and Raquel *didn't* know—until their father's will explained it—was that this "friend" was Queen Elmyr, ruler of the Kingdom of Linevan.

Shannon looked up abruptly. "Does this mean," he breathed, "that Pacifica . . . is the Scrapped Princess?"

Raquel answered in a flat tone, "That's exactly what it means."

The very name "Scrapped Princess" was considered blasphemous throughout the kingdom. Although no one dared whisper it in public, deep in the memories of the Linevan people lived the legend of the infant princess who had vanished, without a trace, at her birth. The rumors about her varied, but almost every one agreed that she'd been killed as an infant.

Shannon quickly went back to the letter.

> *Since I assume that something happened to me, you must protect Pacifica until the day she turns sixteen—the Day of Destiny. I know it's not*

an easy job, and I know that your late mother and I weren't perfect parents . . . but consider this the first and only favor we ever ask of you.

Shannon squinted skeptically. His father had *often* asked for "first and only favors."

P.S. The royal family doesn't know that Pacifica is still alive. If they ever find out, they're sure to send assassins—lots of them. And those bastards from the Church of Mauser will send their own hired killers, too. Just do your best. In the meantime, your mother and I will be spending our time in the afterlife "getting it on," as the kids these days say. Ha ha ha!

"Father," Shannon moaned, massaging his temple. "How the hell can you just spring something like this on us?!"

"Oh, Father." Raquel wept.

Shannon glared at her for a moment, then was overcome with the sudden realization that his being completely unemotional might actually be a bad thing. He wasn't an unfeeling monster, after all.

Regardless, he continued to complain. "I mean, I know this is serious . . . but this is so *like* him, getting others to finish what he started. Like how he left us in a mountain of debt! Why do I have to get stuck with all—?"

A sudden noise interrupted Shannon and caused both siblings to turn abruptly toward the door.

Pacifica leaned against the doorframe, her shoulders sagging.

Shannon blinked. He was the kind of man who could almost supernaturally detect even the quietest interloper, so why hadn't he noticed Pacifica until then? *I guess that letter jarred me more than I thought.*

Pacifica held a piece of paper in her right hand, the shocked look on her face implying that said paper was a separate letter from their father. Pacifica had always known she'd been adopted, but not that she was . . .

"Pacifica," Shannon said as calmly as he could. As if drawn by his call, Pacifica managed to take a cautious step toward him.

Shannon thought of a million things he could say to console her, but the jumble of words in his mind faded before he could choose. Nothing he could say would

change reality—and the wrong words would only make things worse.

He swallowed. "P-Pacifica . . ."

Pacifica's lips parted. She paused a moment, then let out a shrill cry. "That's *Princess* Pacifica to you!"

Shannon chastised himself for being foolish enough to worry, even the slightest, about his little sister.

A few moments later, when things had settled, Shannon walked alone into his parents' former bedroom. Even after ten years, the place still felt exactly the same as when his mother had been alive. Intellectually, Shannon *knew* there was no reason to keep the room as it was—his parents, obviously, no longer needed a place to sleep—but, emotionally, leaving the place intact allowed the room to serve as a sort of shrine to their memory.

He opened the cabinet doors to reveal several wicker-work boxes. Their faded color showed their age; the fine layer of dust on each lid indicated that the boxes had been untouched for some time, and had somehow escaped Raquel's cleaning spree.

"Father," Shannon murmured as he opened the first box, "consider this my inheritance. Or a going-away present—whatever sounds better to you."

His fingers brushed over the dust, and for a moment he was reminded of his own mortality.

Dull-colored armor and gear rested in the boxes, packed with almost ceremonial care. The supplies were evidence of what the husband and wife had been, long before they became shopkeepers. Perhaps a lingering fondness for that lost life had moved the Casulls to keep the strange items for so long.

Shannon unearthed hardened leather armor and related gear, several knives and daggers, gloves and boots reinforced with metal rods, and utility belts for carrying various weapons and equipment. Unfortunately, there were no signs of the most important items: swords, spears, and hatchets. Had his parents disposed of them, or were the weapons stored elsewhere?

"Whatever." Shannon sighed. "I can get some decent weapons from the warehouse, I guess." He began to place pieces of armor out on the floor, then suddenly stopped in surprise.

Before him rested a complete set of Brigadier Model Zero multipurpose hardened leather armor. Having helped out his father for so long, Shannon knew a lot about arms and armor, but he'd never actually seen a

Brigadier Model Zero before. The style had first been adopted by the Linevan Kingdom in Continental Year 5110 for its most elite troops, and although the armor looked simple, it was incredibly intricate in design. But the fact that it took more than ten times longer to craft than ordinary armor led to the Brigadier Model Zero's quick discontinuation.

"I could sell this and buy ten sets of *new* armor," Shannon contemplated aloud, thinking, quite naturally, like the son of a weapons dealer. An insignia embossed in one of the shoulder pads caught his eye.

The Valkyrie.

"Father was in the Mortal Storm?" Shannon shook his head. "That explains his giant arms." Shannon knew only bits and pieces of his foreign father's past, mostly because his father had never liked taking about it.

"And did you know that Mother was a member of the Jade Squadron?"

Shannon had already sensed Raquel's presence behind him and answered without turning, "I had no idea they were such elite soldiers, back in their day."

A bittersweet smile on her face, Raquel knelt beside her brother and opened another box. Its contents included a green robe, various accessories, and daggers. The robe was embroidered with intricate patterns and the words *Jade Squadron* across the breast.

Shannon knew the Jade Squadron was comprised of the palace sorcerers, the most proficient practitioners of magic in the kingdom. Both Shannon and Raquel had learned the basics of magic from their mother, although Shannon had shown a complete lack of aptitude and had stopped his lessons without mastering a single technique.

"I know how you feel," Raquel said quietly. "They acted so silly around us." She ran her fingers across the embroidery. "She was ranked ninth in the squadron."

Shannon frowned. "I don't know. After seeing all this gear . . . I guess what Father wrote about the Scrapped Princess is true."

Raquel turned to her brother with an incredulous glare. "You thought Father was *lying*?"

"Do you know how many times I've fallen for one of Father's pranks? Unlike you, I only believe what I see." He scratched the back of his neck. "All of a sudden, I hear that my sister's some long-lost princess, that her life's in danger, and that I've been promoted to assassin-killing duty. I think I've earned my grain of salt, thanks."

Shannon paused. "Anyway," he said after a moment, "do you think Duke Franki knows about this?"

"I don't know. But like you said, he seems to know something."

"Maybe we should pay him a visit."

"No, no." Raquel pursed her lips disapprovingly. "We can't just waltz in and ask for an audience with the duke. Besides, he's obviously hiding something, so why would he tell us what he knows?"

"I wasn't talking about the front door, Raquel," Shannon explained dryly. "I was planning on doing some sneaking."

Raquel stared at her brother for a moment, surprised, then broke into a wide smile. She ruffled his hair. "You look just like Father when you talk like that," she said fondly.

"Do me a favor and never say that again."

a fateful choice

Sunday was a day of rest for most people in Manurhin, but not for the children of commoners. Sunday was the one day a week children were excused from work to attend the duke-sponsored school. Pacifica, whether she was in the proper state of mind to go or not, had a responsibility to show up.

"Hi, Pacifica," chimed a pretty classmate, strolling into the classroom.

She had long, dark hair, tied back with a white ribbon; she brushed a stray strand behind her ear as she walked alongside Pacifica.

Pacifica didn't bother looking up from the paper in her hand. "Hi," she replied absently as she slumped deeper into her chair.

The classmate stopped. "Pacifica?" she asked as she bent down to get Pacifica's attention. "Something wrong?"

Pacifica folded the sheet and glanced up. The classmate was Miyutia Wesson, Pacifica's deskmate and her best friend at school—and possibly anywhere.

"Is it because of your father?" Miyutia asked.

"No. Er, well . . ." Pacifica frowned, then lowered her head onto her desk. "There's that, too." Pacifica kept her face buried in her arms for a moment, then took a deep breath. "Miyutia," she ventured at last. "If I told you I wasn't really Pacifica Casull, what would you do?"

"Huh?"

Pacifica peeked over her forearm. "Y'know—if I told you I was a . . . princess or something."

Miyutia went silent for a moment. She gave her friend a skeptical look.

"Well," Miyutia answered slowly, "I guess I would tell you to find some professional help for that broken brain of yours."

Pacifica scowled. "Some friend *you* are."

"I'm trying really hard to not laugh at you. Doesn't that count for something?"

"Miyutia!"

Miyutia held out her hands in defeat. "Fine, fine," she said with a smile, swishing into her seat and patting Pacifica on the arm. "I'm sorry. So what's really bothering you? Something in your father's will about your adoption?"

Pacifica frowned again. "Yeah."

"Come on, Pacifica. You always knew you were adopted, why get upset about it now?"

"It's not that. It's just . . ." True, the fact that she'd been adopted—something obvious to anyone who saw her siblings' dark complexions next to Pacifica's blonde hair and blue eyes—had never really troubled Pacifica. She was as much a part of the Casull family as she could be, and that was that.

Pacifica rested her head on her arms. "Since yesterday," she began, "Shannon and Raquel have been acting kinda weird."

"Well, yeah. Your father died, and they have to take over the family business."

"I know that. But it's *more* than that."

Miyutia snapped her fingers. She smiled broadly at Pacifica, tapping her troubled friend right between the eyes. "I get it," Miyutia declared. "You just miss the attention."

Pacifica blinked. "Huh?"

"Your brother and sister are busy and you're lonely. My little brother Andy's the same way—when he doesn't get constant attention, he sulks like a kicked kitten." She smiled. "You're doing the exact same thing, Pacifica. It's actually kinda cute."

Pacifica's jaw dropped. "Hey!" she cried. "What's that supposed t-t-to . . . ?"

"Ha! You're stuttering—that means I'm right!"

Red in the face, Pacifica pushed herself up from her desk. "All right," she snapped, cracking her knuckles. "That's it!"

Miyutia threw up her hands in mock terror. "Help!" she cried. "I'm totally scared of Pacifica!"

The other students watched with mild, bored expressions. This wasn't the first time the two girls had caused a ruckus before class.

Unfortunately, it was at that moment that the teacher walked in. "Pacifica!" she barked, slamming her paperwork on her desk. "Miyutia! If it's all right with you two, I'd like to teach something today."

The students snickered as Pacifica dropped back into her seat and Miyutia folded her hands in her lap.

"Yes'm," the girls chimed in unison.

❧

Harlington Road stretched out under a clear blue sky, its surrounding farmland picked clean by the recent wheat harvest. Harlington was one of seven main roads of Manurhin; to the north it led to a hilly area owned by Duke Franki (and technically off-limits to the public.) Unofficially, however, the locals enjoyed the land, as it was neither fenced in nor guarded—testament, perhaps, of the duke's generous attitude toward the populace.

Shannon walked up the road, complaining to his sister. " 'Sneaking' generally involves the cover of darkness, and a Sunday afternoon has little-to-no darkness."

"This is more practical," Raquel explained. "We can't leave Pacifica home by herself at night, but she's safe in school at the moment. And what does the time of day matter? We're *invisible* now."

Which, indeed, they were. Any passerby would have witnessed their conversation as dialogue between two disembodied voices—a possible catalyst for cardiac arrest.

"I know that." Shannon paused. "I just thought this sort of operation would be more . . . thrilling."

"This way is easier. Don't you like to be at ease?"

Shannon threw out his invisible hands. "Right," he said quickly. "Forget what I said. I want this the easy way."

The spell that masked the siblings was the military magic illusion technique Utgard, a spell that enveloped the conjurer in a 360-degree illusion to allow him or her to blend in with any surroundings. Raquel used Utgard in its most basic form; a sorcerer could also combine the technique with more magic to actually appear as someone else.

If an Utgard spell was generated with too much force, the wall of illusion could block the conjurer's view of the outside world—in other words, a sorcerer had to use the right amount of energy to allow outside light to penetrate the cloak of illusion, while simultaneously keeping light from leaking out. The technique operated on the same principles as a glass window that reflected images. Consequently, the technique's weakness was that the illusion could have visible spots if the conjurer was hit with bright light at the wrong angle, or passed between two areas of different light intensities. Raquel needed to stay focused.

Using the spell at all made Shannon uncomfortable. "This still doesn't feel right," he murmured. "Stealth needs ducking, alertness, panic—that sort of thing. I'm worried the spell's going to make me lazy and cause a stupid mistake."

"You worry too much," Raquel said.

"And you don't worry enough." Shannon crossed his arms. "Considering we shared our mother's womb for so long, you'd think we'd have more in common."

"That would be boring."

But safer, Shannon thought. Raquel could be unpredictable; he was never completely sure *what* she was thinking.

A child passing by stopped and gaped, certain that he'd heard voices. But only two things met his bewildered eyes: the wide road and the painfully bland country scenery.

"Think about it," Raquel went on. "Imagine spending every day with someone who was exactly like you. After a while, it would get depressing."

"I guess, but—"

"You can learn new and exciting things from people who have different opinions."

Shannon paused for a moment. Raquel's voice was as relaxed as it usually was, free of pretensions but very self-assured. He liked that about her.

"You know what?" he said at last.

"Hm?"

"Sometimes you . . . inspire me."

"Do I really?"

Although Shannon couldn't see her, he still felt her smile.

Time to change the subject.

"Anyway," Shannon said with a cough. "We should, uh, be close to Franki Manor by now. Be sure to stay sharp."

"Sharp it is," Raquel chimed, her voice warm.

❦

You're the Scrapped Princess. Those were the last words in Yuma's letter to Pacifica.

He'd outlined (earlier in the note) that Pacifica's older siblings could be pestered for more information,

but the several times Pacifica had gone to Shannon and Raquel, the siblings had simply changed the subject and left Pacifica in the dark.

Pacifica slumped back in her chair and ignored her teacher's droning voice; she had far more important things to think about. The girl took a mental inventory. Everyone had heard of the Scrapped Princess . . . but beyond the name, legends and rumors came in all the colors of the rainbow.

The most common elements of the Scrapped Princess tale were the following:

> *Long, long ago, Queen Elmyr of the Linevan Kingdom gave birth to fraternal twins, a boy and a girl. The 5111th Oracle of Saint Grendel declared the infant girl evil, so the Court had her killed and then pretended she'd never existed. The End.*

Less common embellishments included the rumor that the princess was the incarnation of a mighty demon that had fought Mauser in the Battle of Creation, or that the priests who had heard the Scrapped Princess prophecy had been killed. Of course, it was also said by some that the princess was covered with scales and had deathly stinky feet.

I really don't like that last one, Pacifica thought with a scowl. It was stupid to assume such a thing before smelling the feet in question.

All in all, Pacifica wasn't too worked up over a fifteen-year-old prophecy. After all, the 5111th Oracle of Saint Grendel would have been before Pacifica's birth, and every mention of the Scrapped Princess had been stricken from public record. All that remained were rumors, and who could really worry about rumors?

On the other hand, devout Mauserists considered the name "Scrapped Princess" blasphemous, and even a fair number of non-Mauserists believed that the Scrapped Princess really had been the incarnation of a demon. After all, in the five thousand-plus years since the first Oracle of Saint Grendel, she was the only person a prophecy had specifically ordered exterminated.

"Great," Pacifica murmured under her breath. "I wish I'd never found Father's letter."

The teacher's voice jolted her out of her daydream. "Pacifica Casull, I asked you to read the next part."

Pacifica nearly jumped out of her chair. "Er, yes!" she called as she quickly flipped through her book.

"Chapter four," Miyutia whispered from across the aisle. "Fifth paragraph."

Pacifica shot Miyutia a grateful glance before reading from her textbook in a fairly steady voice.

◦✦◦

In the Linevan Kingdom, the duke of a city or province normally resided in a castle built at the territory's most strategically important location, in order to protect the nobility in times of war. But for Manurhin—a rural, walled city, almost certain to never see battle—a fortress was almost amusingly superfluous. The castle of Manurhin, used by the duke's predecessors, had been abandoned when Duke Franki took power. He instead resided in a modest manor on a hill, set apart from the local council's administrative hall.

A particularly odious guest, sitting in said manor's simple reception room, looked disdainfully around him.

"This place is pretty plain," he pointed out. "It might suit a dying old man, but not the intrepid Duke Franki, former commander of the Royal Third Western Brigade Road Blockers." As if he found something amusing, the man snickered, causing his corpulent form to jiggle a bit. The edges of his mouth stretched into a sneer as his repulsive tongue darted out to moisten his lips.

"What is it that you want?" Duke Franki asked from the other side of the table. Behind the duke stood his female attendant, her body stationary as a rock. "Mister . . . 'Big Shot,' did you say? You came to my home unannounced—was it only to besmirch the good name of Franki Manor?"

"There's no need to be angry," Big Shot assured him insincerely. "Forgive my bad manners. I was educated at Wildy's; I didn't have time to learn etiquette there." He shrugged his shoulders. He thought the gesture looked regal, but the effect was simply crude.

A silent companion sat beside Big Shot, his tall, thin build in stark contrast to the portly slob's. The other man seemed roughly in his late thirties, with long, dark, disheveled hair and hollow eyes. He looked gravely ill, both physically and mentally. He'd made no attempt to remove the dark red cloak from his shoulders.

"I wanted to ask you about something I've been looking into," Big Shot told the duke. "About six days ago, a man died, as you know." Big Shot cast a knowing glance upward.

Duke Franki and the woman remained silent, their expressions betraying nothing.

"I think his name was Yuma Casull," Big Shot added. "He was a foul old man of about fifty. Did you know him?"

Another pause. "He was an acquaintance," Duke Franki murmured at last, suspicion lining his voice.

Big Shot licked his lips again and leaned forward against the table. "And just where did he pick up his . . . *skills*, might I ask?"

The duke narrowed his eyes. "So it was you," he growled. "His body bore several blade wounds. We told the public his death was accidental, but he was very obviously murdered."

Big Shot smiled calmly, a hint of pride in his eyes. "Observant of you, Your Grace. I had a group of experienced killers with me, but he felled seven of them without breaking a sweat. He was more than just a weapons dealer, that's for sure."

"And why do you feel the need to ask questions about the dead?"

Big Shot grinned. "I just want to know who I killed. Out of respect, you could say. But honestly, Your

Grace, the job was suspicious in the first place. Three million cetme to kill one kid, on the condition I don't ask questions?"

Big Shot stretched his mouth into a weak, ugly smile. "I can pin someone as Court material from the way they talk. *And* the brat's father turns out to be a master swordsman. I had two combat sorcerers with me, but he still managed to kill everyone, except for us two." Big Shot gestured to the man sitting beside him.

"Your suspicions are of no concern to me," the duke said flatly. "I am under no obligation to reveal anything to the likes of you."

"I thought you might say that. So I have a proposition, Your Grace." Big Shot's beady eyes squinted with mischief. "Tell me what I want to know, and we'll exterminate the girl and leave town immediately. Otherwise . . ." He shrugged slightly. "We might have to start knocking off some law-abiding taxpayers."

The duke's attendant took an abrupt step forward, her right hand sliding into a pocket under her cloak. The man sitting beside Big Shot jumped up and reached both hands behind his hips.

"Stand down, Finebell," Duke Franki commanded.

Finebell hesitated slightly before complying with her master's command. She looked less than pleased at having to do so.

Big Shot glanced up at his companion. "Easy, Sinner," he said carefully. Although Big Shot was clearly not in charge of the taller man, Sinner nonetheless sat back down in his chair.

Big Shot let out a breath. "Fine," he said, tiredly waving a hand. "I take back what I said. Your lady friend here seems pretty formidable, and we already have a good idea who the snotnose-in-question is. Sinner may not look it, but he's good at detective work."

Big Shot pulled a bundle of papers from his pocket. Both the duke and Finebell noticed the dark red stain on one end; it wasn't hard to guess what Big Shot meant by "detective work."

"Yuma Casull's youngest daughter . . ." Big Shot raised an eyebrow, "she wouldn't happen to be the Scrapped Princess, would she?"

Duke Franki remained silent, so Finebell answered for him.

"The Scrapped Princess is a myth," she said evenly. "If she ever existed at all, she died fourteen years ago."

Big Shot's eyes darkened, and his lips curled into a sneer. "Thanks for the recitation," he growled. "But I wasn't talking to you, girlie—I was talking to your master."

"You will *not* speak to my attendant that way," interrupted the duke as his hand flashed toward Finebell. He held down her left hand, which gripped what looked like the handle of a bladed weapon.

Big Shot let out a breath. "Sorry," he said without a hint of sincerity.

"I've nothing more to say to you. Leave here at once."

Big Shot stood. "As you wish, *Your Grace,*" he drawled as he gave a dramatic bow. Sinner floated up from his chair like a weightless specter.

"Let's go, Sinner—it looks like we're no longer welcome. And the young lady won't drop her rude scowl." Big Shot nodded at the duke. "Thanks for your time, Duke Franki. I hope nothing messy has to happen between us."

With that, the two men turned and left the room. Duke Franki and Finebell kept their eyes fixed on the killers until a servant closed the door.

The object of her hatred gone, Fineball released the grip on her weapon and visibly calmed. "What are you going to do?" she asked quietly of her duke.

"There's nothing *to* do, I'm afraid." Duke Franki shook his head. "We've seen nothing and we know nothing."

"Your Grace?"

"It's unfortunate for Yuma's children, but I don't regard the Oracle of Saint Grendel as lightly as Yuma did. Cutting short the life of a child, as regrettable as that is, is nothing compared to what could happen if the events of the prophecy come to pass."

Finebell let the matter drop. Duke Franki was, after all, the ruler of Manurhin, and with that authority came an obligation to protect the people—even if it meant taking actions that went against his own conscience. If he could save two townspeople by allowing one to die, he would unflinchingly order that single death and take full responsibility for it. It was that strength of will that Finebell admired most about the man.

A knock came at the door. "Enter," said the duke.

The door opened slightly, and the duke's steward— a middle-aged man, who managed the duke's other servants—poked his head in. He was the kind of professional who would treat a multi-headed monster with the utmost courtesy, if that monster were a guest of the house.

"Your Grace," he called calmly, "we have apprehended two intruders."

Duke Franki furrowed his eyebrows. "Intruders?" he repeated.

❧

"How many times do we have to go through this before you *learn*, Raquel?!"

"I'm sorry," Raquel replied. "Are you mad?"

"I'm not mad, just try *thinking* before you act."

Shannon's body was bound from neck to ankles with an almost ridiculous amount of rope. Raquel lay beside him, her body similarly cocooned in restraints. The trussed-up siblings were sprawled uncomfortably in the middle of the duke's courtyard.

"But Shannon," Raquel argued with the barest tinge of a whine, "I generated the Utgard spell in all four directions—front, back, left, and right. I *was* thinking, honest."

Shannon sighed. "Not about the top."

A properly executed Utgard spell hid the caster from all angles, but she'd forgotten about the bird's eye view.

Raquel had never been formally trained as a sorcerer—most of the spells she knew had been pieced together from her mother's notes.

Although she was stringent about testing her spells to make sure they worked, the fact that she was self-taught meant there was always the risk of her overlooking something.

Shannon shifted his tired gaze from Raquel to the four young women in front of him. Each wore a white bonnet, a frilly apron, and a blue dress . . . as well as a long sword at the waist.

Raquel and Shannon had been full of confidence earlier that afternoon. Then, while striding fearlessly into Franki Manor, they'd been spotted by a maid hanging sheets on a second-story balcony.

"I see you've discovered that my maids also serve as guards," called a voice. Shannon and Raquel craned their necks to see Duke Franki and Finebell, their steps matching as they entered the manor's courtyard.

Shannon dropped his gaze. "Uh, thanks for coming yesterday," he mumbled.

"Of course," the duke replied graciously, out of habit. A moment later he remembered to whom he spoke.

" 'Thanks'?" he repeated sharply. "Don't be glib with me, boy. I'll not tolerate such insolence from someone caught sneaking into my home."

"Humility was never my strong point," Shannon admitted with (predictably) little humility.

Duke Franki glared at his two captives. "What exactly were you trying to do here? You could have forced your way past my guards—why did you surrender so easily?"

Shannon decided against answering. Both he and Raquel knew how to size up an opponent—a skill taught by their father—and from their analysis of the situation, they *could* have beaten the maids. But the four women weren't so incapable that the siblings could disarm them without injuring them, and Duke Franki hadn't yet proven himself an enemy. They chose surrender over the possibility of harming innocents.

"You two certainly are daring," the duke said. "As one would expect of Yuma's children. But I demand an answer: why did you come here?"

The duke held out a hand, palm-up. Finebell removed a knife from her cloak and placed it in the duke's hand. Shannon recognized the knife as a custom-made stiletto—a weapon designed for stabbing, often favored by assassins.

The duke stepped toward the bound pair. Shannon flinched as the blade approached his prone body.

In one swift motion, the duke cut through the ropes binding Shannon. As Duke Franki moved to free Raquel, Shannon shrugged off the ropes and got to his feet; the tips of four swords immediately came to rest a hair's breadth away from his neck.

Shannon raised his hands. "I won't try anything."

Duke Franki nodded at the maids. The young women promptly whisked their weapons back into their scabbards.

"I just wanted to ask you a few things," Shannon told the duke as he worked the kinks out of his neck.

Duke Franki helped Raquel shake off her ropes and glanced up at Shannon. "You wish to continue our conversation about your father, I assume."

Shannon nodded. "Father was . . . murdered, wasn't he?"

The duke sighed. "I knew you would find out eventually," he murmured. "I take it he left some sort of will?"

"A dirty one, yes." Shannon rolled his eyes.

The duke half-smiled in sympathy and motioned toward the manor.

"Why don't we continue this discussion inside?" he offered. "I'll have the servants make tea."

❧

Mrs. Ze, Pacifica's third-period math teacher, rapped her pointer loudly against the chalkboard.

"Pacifica!" she snapped. "Would you *please* pay attention?"

Pacifica didn't seem to hear her. The preoccupied girl continued to stare out the window.

For a moment, Mrs. Ze felt her blood boil, but she forced herself to remain calm, since, as a schoolteacher, she'd long ago learned the virtue of patience.

Mrs. Ze had always thought of Pacifica as one of the most polite and well-behaved of her thirty-odd students; the girl had never once ignored her or acted in such a contrary manner until today. *Of course*, Mrs. Ze reminded herself, *the girl's father died six days ago.* Concluding that Pacifica was still grieving in her own way, Mrs. Ze let the matter slide.

Pacifica murmured something under her breath. Mrs. Ze only heard something along the lines of "Shannon and Raquel," so she ignored it and turned back to her chalkboard.

"As I was saying—"

"Missus Ze!" Pacifica chose that moment to shoot her hand into the air.

Mrs. Ze swallowed hard to suppress her aggravation. "Yes, Pacifica?" she answered as pleasantly as she could manage.

"I feel really bad, so I'm going home. Okay?" Without waiting for an answer, Pacifica stuffed her books into her school bag and walked briskly out of the classroom. The class, along with a confused Mrs. Ze, could only watch the girl go in stunned silence.

Mrs. Ze cleared her throat. She was the sort of woman who would normally drag a fleeing student back to class, but a fleeing, *mourning* student? In addition, she didn't want to interrupt her lecture—the parents were already complaining about how far behind the official lesson plan she was.

The teacher sighed in resignation and turned back to the board. "Right, as I was saying . . ."

a fateful CHOICE

After leaving Franki Manor, Big Shot and Sinner proceeded to the east side of town, where Pacifica's school stood. The two had made themselves very familiar with the route she took to and from home.

"Let's see," Big Shot mused as he pulled a map of Manurhin from his bundle of papers. "She'll pass through a relatively deserted area right here," he poked a thick finger at the map, "beyond this group of houses. No one will see anything there."

"We're going to take her alive?" Sinner asked. His voice, when he used it, was soft and ominous.

Indeed, the two professionals didn't need an out-of-the-way place to kill a single girl. They could dispatch her and make it look like an accident in a crowd if necessary.

"That brat is too valuable to kill," Big Shot answered with a sly grin. "She has to be the Scrapped Princess—even her age is right. The royal family would be scandalized if the public ever learned she's alive, and I'm sure they'll pay through the nose for our silence."

He licked his thin lips. "I also hear that a group of army officers and high-ranking bureaucrats are hatching a plot to take over the kingdom and make the royal family nothing but figureheads. I'm sure *those* bastards would pay even *more* for the girl."

"They'll kill the girl and us," Sinner warned.

"Don't worry so much." Big Shot rolled up the map. "We just need to play our cards right."

"You mean to betray our client."

"What do you care?" Big Shot asked with a snort. "Don't you need the money for dear Lynthia's—"

Big Shot suddenly leapt to the side, barely avoiding a silver flash that sliced through the spot where he'd been standing. He caught only a fleeting glimpse of the steel blade as Sinner returned it to its scabbard.

"Don't you *ever* speak my daughter's name again," Sinner hissed through clenched teeth.

Big Shot held up his hands. "N-Now, now," he said as cold sweat leaked through his pores. "There's no need to get testy." He knew the sword stroke hadn't meant to kill, but there had been genuine rage behind it. And Big Shot had once seen Sinner *dismember* a man for telling a crude joke about sweet little Lynthia.

Big Shot cleared his throat. "Just hear me out," he explained. "You, er, need the money, and it won't be cheap to hire—five, was it?—five sorcerers. And Grade 1 sorcerers; those bastards cost an arm and a leg."

Sinner glared at him with clouded eyes. Anyone could see the dangerously twisted mind lurking behind those eyes.

Big Shot smiled. "Of course, considering what great friends we are, I'll gladly act as one of those sorcerers, but that still leaves four. Four Grade 1 sorcerers to perform that kind of operation *in secret*. You're talking a million cetme apiece. Even without sharing our three million with those morons who got themselves killed, you still won't have anywhere near enough."

Despite the "friends" comment, Big Shot's sneering tone betrayed his true feelings for Sinner (or lack thereof). To Big Shot, other people existed only for him to use, and he knew he could get Sinner to do anything just by invoking Lynthia's cause.

"Besides," Big Shot added with a greasy smirk, "you can never have too much money, right?"

But Sinner's attention was elsewhere. "Big Shot," he murmured. "Be quiet and look."

Big Shot turned to follow Sinner's steely black gaze. His own eyes widened.

The blonde hair tied neatly back . . . The petite frame . . . The shining blue eyes, like shimmering pieces of perfect sky.

The girl who marched down the other side of the street was unmistakably Pacifica Casull. Big Shot and Sinner had stalked her for quite some time—the action had alerted Yuma to their presence and cost them their allies in the first place.

"What's she doing here *now?*" Big Shot breathed out. "This couldn't be a trap, could it?"

"There's no sign of a lookout or bodyguard." Sinner's eyes darted up and down the street.

Big Shot swallowed. "All right," he whispered. "Then let's get moving. We can hide behind those houses over there."

"Good."

The two men changed direction and headed toward their target. Pacifica, determination thinning the pretty line of her mouth, continued to stride confidently toward her home.

"Was someone just here?" Raquel asked.

The duke, taking his seat across the table from the siblings, furrowed his brow. The maids had departed at his signal, leaving Finebell to silently prepare the tea (and guard Duke Franki, of course).

"How did you know that?"

"The air's a little warm," Raquel explained. "An empty room is cold in the winter, but less so when people stay in it."

"Impressive." The duke fixed his eyes on Raquel and her brother. "I did have other guests. They left just before you arrived." He paused for a moment, returning to his original train of thought. "Regardless, you wanted to talk about your father?"

Shannon and Raquel nodded.

"Forgive me for being blunt, but there's no way for me to soften this blow." Duke Franki took a breath. "Yes, your father was murdered. The man who did it was a professional killer who calls himself Big Shot. He and his companion sat in this very room a few moments ago."

Shannon's expression hardened into one of cold fury. Without a word he shot up and bunched his fists, his eyes burning with a murderous rage.

"What?" he hissed.

Raquel, still in her chair, rested a hand on her brother's arm. She led him back down to his seat.

"Duke Franki," Raquel said in a tone that lacked her usual cheeriness. "Does that mean you're on the same side as those killers?"

Duke Franki kept his eyes locked with Raquel's for a moment, then sighed and looked away.

"You may not believe me," he murmured, "but no. I did, however, receive a letter ten days ago—a letter bearing the official seal of the Royal Chamberlain, and one that even the two killers know nothing about. It instructed me to not hinder those men in any way."

Raquel sat in stunned silence. Shannon simply continued to glare daggers.

"What I'm about to tell you I learned from my own personal sources, so you need not believe it all. But will you at least stay and listen? Your sister is safe at school—I doubt those men would attempt to force their way into such a place."

Raquel thought for a moment, then nodded. The duke folded his hands on the table.

"Approximately one month ago, a lady of the Court was investigated by palace officials for stealing money from the royal treasury to pay off her husband's debts. Soon after her arrest, the Jade Squadron conducted an interrogation, using mind-scanning sorcery to gain evidence of the crime. While searching her memories, however, they happened upon one that shook the foundations of our entire world."

The duke paused. "Fourteen years ago," he said slowly, "this lady of the Court was instructed by the queen to transfer an infant girl out of the palace and into the arms of a waiting couple. But this was no ordinary infant—she was the queen's newly born daughter, a princess."

"The Scrapped Princess," Raquel offered.

The duke nodded. "The uncovering of this secret triggered a series of punishments throughout the palace. After all, the official records state that the infant princess was killed long ago by the palace guards—the Anvar Knights—and that the Jade Squadron burned the body to ashes, sealed it in an urn, and cast it into the Valley of Glass."

The cruelty of the execution slowed the duke's words. Even mass-murderers weren't disposed of in such a manner.

"When this woman's memories revealed that the Scrapped Princess had actually lived, everyone who had overseen her death was punished in secrecy, including the leaders of the Anvar Knights and the Jade Squadron. Some were merely dismissed from the Court; others were stripped of their titles and executed. Altogether, over sixty people were punished because of the scandal.

"Needless to say, the head conspirator, Queen Elmyr, couldn't be put to death. She's been confined to a home on the palace grounds under the terms of house arrest. Furthermore, the Royal Chamberlain has decided to have the central figure in the whole affair—the princess— assassinated before the matter becomes public."

The duke at last went silent. Raquel, one hand still gently gripping Shannon's elbow, cleared her throat. "Duke Franki," she asked, "did you know about this all along?"

The duke scowled bitterly. "I have seen nothing and heard nothing," he said mockingly. Then his expression softened slightly.

"Such ignorance was necessary to allow your family to settle in this city. As a member of the aristocracy of the Linevan Kingdom, I couldn't knowingly help anyone harboring the Scrapped Princess . . . but your father saved my life back in my Road Blocker days, so I accepted Pacifica's forged residency records as my way of returning the favor."

Raquel glanced at her brother. They'd both just heard the duke admit to treason.

"To be honest," the duke said evenly, "I'm not as skeptical as your parents were about the Oracle of Saint Grendel. History shows that the predictions have been wrong only twice. *Twice*, out of more than five thousand prophecies. That translates into almost infallible accuracy."

Every year, the prophecy of Saint Grendel was revealed at Saint Grendel's Cathedral, the main center of the kingdom's official Mauserism faith. Five priests entered five special chambers to hear the Holy Words spoken by the god Mauser, though no one—not even the High Priest himself—knew how or from where the Holy Words were transmitted. Of course, the "words" of Mauser were completely unlike those spoken by man.

The Holy Words were implanted into the priests' minds simultaneously, and these priests, also known as oracles, translated the Holy Words into human speech. After receiving said Holy Words, the oracles conferred in a separate room to decide on a single version to present to the public.

The ceremony occurred every year without change until the 5111th Oracle of Saint Grendel. For the first time in recorded history, the priests failed to emerge from the chambers at the appointed time and the crowd that had gathered was forced to wait. When the screaming began, and the five doors opened to reveal their dying occupants, the priests barely managed to deliver the prophecy:

> *The infant girl must be destroyed. Of the twin children whom the queen shall bear, thou shalt kill the female. Ten and six years from the day of her birth she will bring forth the Day of Destiny and destroy the world; she will demolish order and usher in chaos. She is evil. Thou shalt destroy her.*

Naturally, the palace was thrown into pandemonium, and a fierce debate erupted over the veracity of the prophecy. King Balterik Linevan and his wife, the newly pregnant

Queen Elmyr, resisted violently. It was the first time in history that the prophecy had ever ordered the people to *do* something—some opposed the Oracle on the basis of its unique nature, whereas others claimed the order was proof of a grave danger facing the world.

Nevertheless, the prophecies had proven themselves true too many times for anyone to ignore. Before the palace could agree on an official course of action, Queen Elmyr gave birth to twins—a boy and a girl, just as the Oracle had predicted.

The birth of twins was considered reason enough to believe the prophecy. Before the baby girl could be named or even held once by her father, she was supposedly destroyed.

The incident was erased from all official records, and the public was told that the queen gave birth to a single child, Prince Forcis. Even the prophecy itself was rewritten to sound innocuous. Rumors, of course, still persisted and spread, and the legend of the tragic Scrapped Princess became a staple throughout the kingdom.

"I do pity your sister," the duke admitted as he took a cup of tea from Finebell. "But in view of the prophecies' proven accuracy, I cannot blame those who wish her dead. That's why I've decided to remain neutral in the matter."

"Of course," Shannon said through clenched teeth as he rose to his feet. "Thank you . . . for . . . the information."

He made for the door. Raquel got up to follow, but the duke stopped them with a question. "Do you realize the future you've chosen for yourselves?"

Shannon didn't bother turning. "Excuse me?" he asked darkly.

"You still have another option—you can leave Pacifica to her fate."

Shannon looked over his shoulder, his eyes glittering with fury. "You want me to . . ." He trailed off, ground his teeth, and tried again. "You want me to *let* those bastards kill my little sister?"

"She's not your real sister." The duke's voice quieted a bit as he said, "You and Raquel are about to throw away your lives for her, and your only rewards will be misfortune and death. The palace will pursue her relentlessly. The Oracle will prove true when the very existence of your sister results in the deaths of many—hired killers, you, even innocent civilians. Do you honestly think Pacifica will be happy, surrounded by the corpses of those who died so she could live?"

Shannon and Raquel said nothing.

A hesitant look flashed across Duke Franki's face, as if guilt momentarily gripped him. "If Pacifica Casull dies," he murmured, "the entire problem will be settled."

Shannon couldn't take it. He spun around and rushed at the duke, his sword ripped out of his sheath before he took the first step.

"Finebell!" Duke Franki commanded. "Stop!"

Finebell froze, her raised stiletto—aimed at Shannon—poised in her ready hand. Raquel stood a short distance away, her palm pointed directly at the woman. It was clear what would happen if Finebell interfered.

Shannon crossed the room in three quick strides and pushed his blade against the duke's neck. "What kind of a man *are* you?" Shannon hissed.

Duke Franki stared directly into Shannon's hate-filled eyes. "If mankind could live according to ideals," he said flatly, "there would be no wars. Children would not starve, and the old would die with dignity. But we *don't* live in a perfect world—we're constantly forced to make choices, sometimes between evils. So, I ask you again,

Shannon Casull, is what you are about to do worth the harm it may cause?"

Shannon spat on the floor. "*Worth* isn't the point."

"It's precisely the point."

"You son of a—"

Shannon was interrupted by rapid footsteps from the hallway. The commotion had apparently alerted the guards.

"Shannon!" Raquel shouted as she ran for a nearby wall. Shannon deliberated a moment, his shaking blade still kissing the duke's skin, before finally pulling back. He sprinted to Raquel's side just as she finished chanting a spell.

"Power of Gungnir, release!"

A shockwave spell burst from Raquel's palms, punching a hole in the wall. The Gungnir spell, a Class 1 attack, was designed to destroy any defense—or in Raquel's case, any wall that stood between her and freedom.

In the ensuing cloud of dust, Raquel and Shannon ducked through the hole and ran outside.

"Thanks for the tea!" Raquel called over her shoulder as she and her brother fled.

A group of armed servants poured into the room.

They were led by the duke's steward. All members of the duke's staff had at least *some* weapons training, and roughly half of them were ex-soldiers who had served under the man in the Road Blockers.

"They're getting away!" the steward barked. "Altair, Batille, deploy to the right! Colleen, Deliah, go left, down the passageway! Everyone else—"

"Let them go," the duke ordered.

The servants all stopped what they were doing, while Duke Franki watched the fleeing siblings shrink into the distance.

"But, Your Grace—"

"I was once young and reckless, too," the duke said listlessly. "Although I paid a heavy price for that."

The steward, Finebell, and the older servants lowered their eyes. They knew to what the duke referred.

"They're capable of accepting the consequences of their actions. Let them do as they wish. Besides, I don't want you getting hurt. "They're the children of Yuma and Carol Casull, after all."

Duke Franki slowly stood. As he looked around the room, his gaze fell on the damaged wall.

His mouth curved into a frown. "Reckless indeed," he muttered. "I rather liked that wall."

a tomb for the Lost princess

P acifica sighed and crossed her arms. "Great," she snapped. "Now what?"

After reaching her home, she'd come to discover that Shannon and Raquel were out. She had no idea where they were.

"What's the point in getting out of school early if I just sit here, waiting?" she complained aloud. Pacifica had the unfortunate habit of acting without thinking, and she was once again paying for it. She irritably brushed a stray strand of hair behind her ear and stepped out onto the front lawn.

Before her squatted her arch nemesis.

"Desert Eagle?" she asked the hen. "Do you know where Shannon and Raquel went?"

Of course, the bird didn't answer. She just glared at Pacifica with her sinister little eyes.

Pacifica glared back. "Don't give me that look," she warned. "You've got a lot of attitude for a bird with just one talent. Why don't you do us all a favor and lay your stupid eggs?"

Pacifica turned her attention from the chicken to her empty home. "Whatever," she huffed. "I'll just . . . go for a walk, I guess."

Having decided on her thoroughly unproductive course of action, Pacifica made her way to the back gate and swung it open. She had just closed it behind her when a voice called out.

"Hey, Pacifica!"

Pacifica looked over her shoulder. A middle-aged man of average height and weight trotted up to her, his steps quick and his face anxious.

Pacifica recognized him—he was Miyutia's father, Dan Wesson. Pacifica knew him from the many times he had brought his carpentry tools to the shop for repairs.

But something wasn't right. "Mister Wesson?" Pacifica asked, squinting her eyes. "Are you okay? Your voice sounds funny."

Wesson blinked. "Oh," he said quickly. "I, uh . . . I have a cold." He cleared his throat.

"That's too bad—you should stay home and get some rest."

"I wish I could, but I'm just so busy. Oh, and I'm sorry about your father."

Pacifica looked away. "Thank you," she said quietly. "I'm doing a lot better now." Her father's death still pained her, but the new developments with his letters were distracting her from the grief.

"Aren't you a tough one? Yep, I suppose we all have to move on eventually." He glanced at the store. "Do you know what you're doing with the shop yet?"

Pacifica shrugged. "I guess my big brother's taking over. But Father always did the inventory by himself, so we haven't figured everything out yet."

"I see. Well, I hope you can help me." Wesson rubbed his chin. "I left a tool here to be repaired, but I'm afraid I need it back as soon as possible. I don't mind if it's not fixed yet."

"Um . . . I don't know where anything is in there, and Shannon and Raquel are out."

"Are they?" Wesson asked as he raised his eyebrows. He gestured somewhere behind him. "I actually saw Shannon on my way here. He looked like he was in a hurry, so I didn't say hi."

Pacifica immediately grew interested. "You saw him? Where?"

"He was heading north on Richardson Street."

Richardson Street had originally been built as the main road to the old Castle Franki. Once a heavily traveled thoroughfare, the street had eventually grown as deserted as the castle.

Pacifica groaned. "Why would he go *there*? Ugh." She glanced up at Wesson. "Was my sister with him?"

"I can't really say. I just caught a glimpse of him from a distance, you know." Wesson rubbed his chin again. "I mean, I could help you go find him, if that would speed things up a bit."

"Good idea." Pacifica quickly locked the gate behind her. "It's better than just waiting here."

Wesson smiled, something sinister curling at the edges of his lips. "It is," he agreed smoothly.

a tomb for the Lost princess

The assassins were somewhere in town. If they were professionals, Shannon and Raquel knew the men would avoid the school because it would be difficult to blend in there. If the palace wanted secrecy, the killers would wait until Pacifica finished her classes.

Unfortunately, she'd left school early today.

"She said she didn't feel well," Mrs. Ze explained, suspiciously eyeing the siblings' outfits. Their cloaks couldn't hide the combat gear underneath. Shannon's hardened leather armor, although not as bulky as its metal counterpart, still made him look a few sizes larger, and both he and his sister wore long swords at their waists. If the teacher hadn't known them, she would have thought them robbers or kidnappers.

"What do you *mean* she went home?!" Shannon shouted. The muscles in his neck tightened. "When?!"

The teacher shrunk back. "Well . . . before noon, I think. It wasn't that long after class started."

"Thank you," Raquel said politely.

As Shannon spun to leave, Mrs. Ze called out to Raquel before the girl could follow suit.

"By the way, Miss Casull." Mrs. Ze crossed her arms. "Pacifica's scores in math have fallen lately. She needs to complete one unit a day, *every* day. It's important for her to hear that from family members."

Raquel nodded. "I'll be sure to mention it to her," she said gravely.

Shannon lost what little patience he had left. "NO PARENT-TEACHER CONFERENCES!" he roared as he gripped the back of Raquel's neck and physically marched her toward the classroom door. "We're leaving!"

Mrs. Ze jumped as he slammed the door shut behind them. Muttering to herself about common courtesy, she wondered what could have possibly rubbed Shannon the wrong way.

Pacifica was the one who decided to skip class, she thought ruefully. *As if I could chain an orphaned girl to her seat.*

❧

Pacifica looked up at the deserted castle. "Ew," she commented with disgust. "What would Shannon want in a creepy place like this?"

The building was old—almost six hundred years old, according to hearsay. It had been solidly designed and built, but it was choked with vines and the cracked stone walls were covered with moss. The castle, abandoned by the people it had been built to protect, looked and felt as dead as its former occupants.

"He's not the one who came here for something," Wesson called from behind.

Puzzled by the mocking tone in Wesson's voice, Pacifica glanced over her shoulder. The carpenter smiled at her—a threatening, condescending smile.

She blinked. "What's that supposed to mean?" she asked.

"*I'm* the one collecting, sweetheart." His eyes glittered. "And I'm only interested in you."

Ice shot through Pacifica's veins. In an instant, everything became frightening clear.

"N-No," she breathed as she stumbled back a step. "You're not . . . this isn't . . ."

Like Shannon, Pacifica didn't completely believe the story of her origin. After all, she'd always lived the ordinary life of an ordinary shopkeeper's daughter; who could honestly believe that she was some sort of poison to the world?

But as she stared at the carpenter, his form growing wavy right before her eyes, a horrible lump of sudden fear lodged itself right in her throat.

"M-Mister Wesson?" she croaked.

Wesson vanished completely, only to be replaced by a bigger, corpulent man. It was another use of the Utgard spell.

Big Shot smiled his greasy smile.

"Too naïve to mistrust a soul," he chided with a little shake of his head. "Or was my acting that good? Whatever the case, it's true what they say—the cuter they are, the dumber they turn out."

Pacifica swallowed hard and clenched her fists. "Who are you?" she asked as bravely as she could.

Big Shot gave an exaggerated bow. "Big Shot at your service, little one. I'm a professional eliminator, what the common folk call a hired killer." His lips curled into a smirk. "I offed your daddy, Princess."

Pacifica went pale. "You . . . you killed . . ."

"Well, he *did* kill seven of my men, so I guess that makes us even. They were expendable, but they still cost me plenty." Big Shot winked creepily. "Don't take it so personally. You're the Scrapped Princess—plenty of people want you dead, so it's only natural there'd be some casualties of war."

"No!" Pacifica shouted as she fought the chill overcoming her. "This whole thing is crazy! I didn't *do* anything! Why should I have to die?!"

"Unfortunately, my dear, the choice between life and death isn't always ours." He shrugged. "My dead companions didn't want to die. Neither did your father. And as long as you live, people will keep dying—your existence itself is a sin against Mauser."

Pacifica's mouth opened, but no sound came out. She felt her knees go weak.

Big Shot's greasy tone turned even greasier. "You're scared," he drawled. "I can see that. And who wouldn't be? I'd be scared if I knew I could cause the deaths of more people I cared about. Like a friend, a loved one . . ." He raised an eyebrow. "Or a big brother or sister?"

Pacifica forced herself to breathe. *People are dying because of me?* she managed to think through the whirling fog in her mind. *Father was killed . . . because of me?*

Did that mean Miyutia was in danger? Were Shannon and Raquel? The very thought of her friends and family getting hurt for her sake turned Pacifica's stomach.

"J-Just my being alive is doing this?" she unintentionally asked aloud.

Big Shot took a careful step forward. "That's right," he said, egging her on. "You should've never been born. You're the Scrapped Princess, prophesied as the one to destroy the world."

Pacifica gripped her shaking arms. She hadn't thought much about the danger of being the Scrapped Princess. After mulling over her origin, she'd come to one conclusion: her parents had still raised her, so things *couldn't* be that bad. If the Casulls had loved her, could she really be a curse?

But now her mother and father were gone. Not only that, but they were probably dead because of Pacifica's very existence. And her brother and sister were in danger.

Pacifica's fingertips turned white. She couldn't lose Shannon and Raquel—they were everything to her.

"You can't go on as Pacifica Casull," Big Shot warned. "You're the Scrapped Princess, an abandoned child and a living sin. But I can help you." His voice, a little gentler now, took on a convincing lilt. "I've prepared a vessel to contain you. You're not going to die in it; it's just to hold you, since your existence still has a value. And I can help you get revenge against the royal family—the family that abandoned you in the first place."

Pacifica took another shaky step back. *Vessel?* she wondered.

"Come on, little princess." Big Shot, to match her movement, took another step forward. "I just told you I'm not going to kill you, so what are you afraid of? Take my offer while you can. The entire world's after you, and not everyone's as sweet as me."

Pacifica swallowed. To a girl who had been forsaken and left with no future and no hope, Big Shot's offer sounded almost worth taking. And if he took her away, all the people she loved in Manurhin would be out of danger. And yet . . . it would mean washing away the past fourteen years of her life. The love her family had shown her, the memories they'd shared . . . it would all fade away.

"N-No," Pacifica blurted. She swallowed again, then quickly shook her head. "I-I'm not going."

"Are you sure about that?"

Pacifica gritted her teeth. She'd been Pacifica Casull her entire life—she'd only been the Scrapped Princess for a day. She wasn't going to throw everything away yet, whether her fate was sealed or not.

"Get . . . get away from me, you dirty pig."

Big Shot sighed. "That's too bad," he said with a hum. "Your cooperation would've made things easier, but now I'll have to use a mind-control spell on you." He raised his hand in Pacifica's direction. "A *very* strong one that can never be undone."

Of the many types of mind-control spells, several were designed to last permanently. Such spells were imprinted onto the victim's mind, and when such an internalized spell was used on someone who had no natural abilities in sorcery—or hadn't been trained to defend against subconscious attacks—the spell could fuse with the victim's mind irreversibly.

In the worst cases, the spirit was destroyed, leaving the victim an empty shell that would only respond to commands.

"Here we go," Big Shot murmured as his lips curled into a smile.

"No!" Pacifica screamed. She bolted back in the direction of town, hoping to get to where someone could hear her.

But Big Shot was ready. "O Laevatein!" he called. "Wand of Fire, ignite!"

A ball of fire exploded in front of Pacifica, sending the screaming girl hurtling through the air. Big Shot, guessing Pacifica might try to escape, had readied the spell in advance. The thick growth of weeds cushioned Pacifica's fall, but the impact still knocked the wind out of her. She lay gasping on the ground.

Big Shot licked his lips. "Where do you think you're going?" he drawled as he advanced slowly, his gloating smile reminiscent of a sadistic predator's. "The entire *world* is against you. There's no one to protect you, no one to take you in. Pacifica Casull has become nothing more than the Scrapped Princess." He laughed, his fat shaking with the movement. "What a sad story! Ha ha ha!"

Pacifica panted, trying desperately to catch her breath. "Th-that's what *you* think," she hissed as she staggered to her feet. She stumbled in the direction of the castle, one arm wrapped around her stomach.

Big Shot laughed again. "You idiot!" he called after her. "There's no way out over there!"

Pacifica knew that. She knew the killer could trap her on the grounds of the abandoned castle, but there was nowhere else to run. And she couldn't take another moment of Big Shot's disgusting arrogance.

"Come and get me," she growled as she fled through the weeds and toward the crumbling fortress.

❦

Sinner dreamed.

His daughter stood before him: sweet, precious Lynthia, the only person in the world who meant anything to him. She smiled at him, her young face radiant with joy. Her flaxen hair—inherited from her father—blew in the breeze, and her mother's blue eyes sparkled in her lovely face. He reached out to hold his beloved child in his arms.

But before he could touch her, she suddenly vanished. He searched everywhere for her, panicking as he ran through a hostile landscape, but she was nowhere to be found.

He suddenly saw a figure in the far distance. He ran desperately toward it, hoping beyond hope . . . but it was an adult woman, with sharp blue eyes. Sinner's traitorous wife. Sinner demanded she bring him to Lynthia, but the woman refused. He drew his sword, and in one smooth motion sliced off her head.

He suddenly noticed a small figure on the ground behind his wife's corpse. It was his daughter; her hair was stringy and stuck to her forehead, her face deathly pale. Her eyes were closed, as if she slept, but no amount of shaking or yelling could rouse her. He knelt beside her, begging her to speak.

A man appeared. He was dressed as a doctor, and his voice was full of condemnation. "She's dying, Sinner," he boomed. "She's dying because of you!"

Sinner jerked awake. Panting, his eyes flew around to take in his surroundings.

The man lay in a bed in his makeshift room at Castle Franki. He quickly checked to make sure his daughter was safely beside him; she lay there as she had in his dream, pale and thin and sadly unresponsive. Sinner sighed. Passing a hand over her hair, he slowly sat up.

Lynthia had been a lively and energetic child, quick to pout when things didn't go her way, but faster to smile when life was kind. Sinner had raised her by himself. It had been difficult, but he loved her with all his heart.

For a while, he had loved Lynthia's beautiful mother, too. But Sinner's lifestyle had required him to often leave her side, and during his absences her heart began to stray. One day he returned home to find his wife gone. She didn't leave so much as a note—only their infant daughter.

In a rage, he searched for the woman. It took him only a week to track her down and find her with a younger lover. Enraged at what he saw, he hacked them both to pieces.

He told Lynthia that her mother had died of an illness, hoping to shield the child from the harsh reality of her mother's betrayal. He raised Lynthia with all the love he had. He would have gladly fought the entire world to protect her . . . but he couldn't do battle with a disease, and it was a disease that was taking her away.

She had been only five years old at the onset of her worrisome symptoms. Sinner had brought her to a doctor, and the news had been like a knife to his heart—she was dying, and there was no way to stop it. But Sinner didn't give up hope. He took her to another doctor, then another, but the answer was always the same. No physician could stop a disease built into her body. She had had it since birth; she had inherited it from her father.

a tomb for the Lost princess

Sinner, of course, was healthy despite the curse. Sometimes he wondered if Lynthia's illness was punishment for all the murders he'd committed. He screamed at the heavens, begging whatever god or devil might be listening, to let him die in her place. Silence was his only answer.

And yet there was still a shred of hope. In his search for a cure, he had come across a spell that could be used to transfer a personality from one body to another. It had only been performed successfully a few times, and it was strictly forbidden on the continent because of the necessary destruction of the soul residing in the "new" body. But Sinner didn't care much for rules, nor did he have qualms about killing. He would gladly go to hell if it meant saving his innocent daughter.

Sinner pushed his legs over the side of the bed. Soon he'd have the money to hire the sorcerers, he reminded himself as he slid his feet into his boots. Soon his daughter would open her eyes; soon she would call his name once again.

Sinner stood. He gazed down at the child in his bed, her tiny body very still. He paused, silent, before reaching for his cloak. *Soon.*

"Where the hell *is* she?!" Shannon slammed his fist against the side of his house. "Dammit, Pacifica!"

Shannon and Raquel had searched everywhere they could think of, but Pacifica was nowhere to be found. One of the neighbors had seen Pacifica leave the house with a man; unfortunately, this neighbor hadn't seen whom the man was, or where the two had gone.

"Raquel, what about the Explorer spell?!"

"There's no way I could pull off a wide-area search spell on my own," Raquel replied with a shake of her head. She'd already tried every search spell she knew, but she'd had no luck finding Pacifica within their limited ranges. Explorer had a much larger range, but it required two sorcerers: one to cast the base spell, and one to amplify the first sorcerer's energy. Raquel was quite powerful—as measured by the sorcerer's capacity index, or SCI, she had three times the magic capability of an average sorcerer—but even with her level of power, there was only so much she could do by herself.

"I could help you," Shannon suggested.

"A search spell has to be executed with a high degree of precision; you couldn't manage it. Besides, we're not even sure anything happened to Pacifica."

"How can you act so calm?!" he practically shrieked. "Aren't you worried?!"

"Of course I'm worried," Raquel retorted, sounding a little hurt. "That doesn't make it any less true."

Shannon sighed. Rubbing his eyes, he murmured, "I'm sorry."

Raquel watched her brother thoughtfully. "Shannon," she asked after a moment, "are you thinking about what Duke Franki said? You know, about—"

"Of course not!" He cut her off abruptly. "There's nothing to think about!"

Shannon honestly hadn't given the "choice" a second thought since they'd left the duke's manor. He had to protect Pacifica. It didn't matter if the world hated him for his decision, or even if it cost him his life. Pacifica was his sister—blood or no—and he wouldn't abandon her.

He kicked the wall angrily.

"You two seem to have a real problem with violence toward buildings," a woman's voice called out.

The siblings turned.

Finebell walked calmly and gracefully through the open back door.

Shannon and Raquel immediately took a step back, shifting into fighting stances.

Finebell shook her head. "I didn't come here for a battle—I was simply asked to make a delivery." She pulled a piece of paper from her pocket and handed it to Shannon. "It's a bill for the damage at Franki Manor."

Shannon stared at the paper like it had sprouted heads. "You're *kidding* me!" he screamed. "At a time like this?!"

Finebell ignored his rage and turned to leave. After taking a few steps, she paused to glance back.

"By the way. We heard rumors recently about strange activity at the old Castle Franki, so last night our steward created a surveillance field around the perimeter. A little while ago, it detected three intruders—one of them a teenage girl."

After saying her piece, Finebell left the house. Raquel and Shannon looked at each other in shock. Shannon ran to follow the duke's bodyguard, but stopped at the sight of something leaning against the stone wall. It definitely hadn't been there earlier.

Shannon picked up the item. It was a sword, larger than average and single-bladed; Shannon knew it as a *tachi*. Tied to the scabbard was a tag with the words IMPORTANT EVIDENCE written next to a stamp of the duke's seal.

"This . . . this is Father's," Shannon breathed.

It was the sword Yuma had held in his last moments—the sword with which he'd defended his youngest daughter's life. Gripping the weapon firmly, Shannon ran out onto the road.

"Hey!" he yelled at Finebell's retreating form. "If you want to return something, do us all a favor and learn to be direct!"

Raquel chuckled. "Oh, Shannon," she murmured. "If everyone were as direct as you, nobody would hear over the yelling."

⚫

The inside of Castle Franki wasn't nearly as run-down as its exterior. The building had been made of stone and brick to protect its occupants in times of war, so it had a reassuring sturdiness far beyond that of a house or manor. Of course, the walls were dirty and cracked, and all that remained of its rich furnishings were scraps of wood and fabric strewn across the floor, but its sheer size still conveyed the wealth and power of those who had built it.

"What a fitting place for a Scrapped Princess," Big Shot called through the dead halls of the castle. His voice echoed so loudly that Pacifica couldn't tell where it came from.

He probably doesn't think I stand a chance because I'm a kid, she thought from her hiding spot behind a pillar. She hated to admit it, but the man was right—her father had taught her some basic self-defense techniques, but they would be useless against a hired killer who knew sorcery.

"You'd better take care, Highness," Big Shot warned. "The castle's crumbling. You never know when it might fall on you."

Before the sound of his voice died out, a loud explosion rocked the castle. The deafening reverberation from Big Shot's attack spell engulfed Pacifica, as chunks of stone rained down from the ceiling. She let out a panicked scream.

Big Shot turned in the sound's direction.

"Thank you," he called cheerfully. "Now just stay where you are."

Pacifica bit her lip and vowed to not repeat her mistake. Swallowing, she crept away from the voice as silently as she could. Another explosion rocked the castle, but she just clenched her fists and fought to keep her balance in the darkness.

Her mind raced. She *had* to find a way back to town—Big Shot was a professional killer, so he wouldn't follow her into a crowded place. But how could she get out? All the doors and windows of the castle were boarded up tightly to keep out animals and vagrants. The walls were deteriorating, but not so badly that a petite person like Pacifica could smash through them. She was practically *sealed* in a giant dungeon.

The only brightness in her world—literally—was the sunlight that leaked through the window slats, providing barely enough light for Pacifica to pick her way through the dark.

I have to hide, she thought. *I can wait until he passes me, then run for the front door.*

Of course, that particular plan was risky, so she also contemplated just staying out of Big Shot's reach until

Shannon and Raquel came to save her. *Shannon and Raquel will come, won't they?*

Pacifica's heart sank. She was . . . she was the Scrapped Princess now. She couldn't forget that. Everyone said she was going to destroy the world, and that world included Shannon and Raquel. Did that mean that when they helped her, it was like killing themselves?

Pacifica had never doubted her relationship with her older siblings. Maybe Shannon sighed when she said she needed him, and maybe Raquel wasn't always paying attention, but when trouble reared its ugly head, they had always come to Pacifica's rescue.

But what about now? Why would they help me now, if I'm only going to hurt people?

Her knees began to shake. She felt ashamed for expecting so much of them. She hated the idea of her brother and sister risking their lives for her sake . . . but at the same time, she couldn't stand the thought of never seeing them again. She longed for them. She wanted them so badly it hurt.

Pacifica took a breath.

She still believed in them. How could she not, after all they'd always done for her? Even if her carefree life with her family was indeed over, she couldn't accept that they'd betray her. She couldn't and she wouldn't.

I'm waiting for you, she silently warned her siblings. *And if you don't come, my ghost'll haunt you for the rest of your lives. I'll come into your bedrooms and spook you every night!*

Using her defiant thoughts to keep her spirits up, Pacifica pressed on through the dim light.

The layout of the castle was complex, yet Pacifica had few escape routes: many of the passageways were boarded up, and she avoided small rooms in an effort to keep moving.

Unfortunately, she knew that Big Shot had probably *also* realized her predicament, and was likely getting sick pleasure out of chasing her into a corner. She shivered at the thought of him licking his greasy lips.

Just when she thought she'd reached a dead end, Pacifica noticed a white light shining at the end of a dim hallway. It was far brighter than the weak flickers coming through the gaps in the window boards.

An opening!

Like a drowning woman struggling for the water's surface, Pacifica desperately made for the light. She barely managed to stay on her feet as she stumbled through the mysterious doorway. Panting and gripping her knees, Pacifica looked up.

She was in what looked like a large chapel. Mammoth stained-glass windows loomed on every wall, but most of the colored glass had been broken long ago. Other than a raised altar, there was nothing but a wide, flat floor in the spacious room.

A lone man bathed in fragmented colored light sat at that altar. He wore a blue- and white-striped cloak around his abnormally thin frame. He sat hunched away from Pacifica. Cradling something against his chest, he rocked gently back and forth.

Pacifica gasped.

"It's the Scrapped Princess," the man said without looking up. His voice was soft and chilling.

Pacifica felt panic grip her. "Wh-Who are you?" she squeaked, although she knew it was a stupid question. It was obvious that the man was somehow connected to Big Shot.

"Sinner," he said evenly, "though there's no need for you to remember that." He rose as if weightless, and the light reached the bundle in his arms.

Pacifica didn't realize what the bundle was at first. More accurately, an instinct deep inside her stopped her from *trying* to recognize the shape. But like a slow-acting poison, realization crept through her, filling her veins with ice. She squeezed shut her eyes and released a blood-curdling scream.

Sinner cradled the decomposing body of a small child.

∽✧∽

Playtime's over, Big Shot thought with a grin. He knew Pacifica's scream meant she'd run into Sinner, and that meant he was one step closer to payday.

The thrill of victory giving him speed, Big Shot hurried along the corridor. He needed to get there before the girl said the wrong thing. The last thing Big Shot needed at that point was his prey getting sliced to ribbons by his insane colleague.

A blinding light suddenly flashed at his feet. Big Shot, his eyes wide, dove to the side.

An explosion of flame engulfed the spot where he'd been standing. The man rolled to safety, his cloak narrowly avoiding the far-reaching licks of the flame.

Blinking against the blistering hot air, he stared at the fading sparks in surprise.

It was Laevatein—the same spell he'd used earlier—only far, far more powerful.

Big Shot scrambled to his feet and turned. He could just make out the form of a young woman standing in the shadows.

"Raquel Casull," Big Shot called arrogantly. "You're more than a little late."

Raquel took a step forward. "And I'm guessing you're the killer?" she asked. "I'm sorry, but I'm afraid I'm going to have to take you out."

Big Shot sneered in response. "I don't think you understand who you're dealing with, girl. I'm a professional assassin, and a sorcerer who fought battles before you could wipe your—"

"People of the flames, dance!"

Big Shot's rant was cut off as a fiery explosion tossed him into the air. He yelped.

Invisible hands dragged him into the air.

Raquel had cast Muspell, an active defense spell which was usually employed against a large group of attacking opponents.

Although the explosion it produced wasn't commonly fatal, the physical pain it caused was punishment enough.

Big Shot gurgled a cry as his body slammed into the wall. After sliding to the floor, he clenched his fists and shakily tried to stand.

"Why, you little—"

"People of the flames, dance!"

This time several consecutive explosions tossed Big Shot back and forth, eliminating his chance to counterattack or even regain his footing.

"W-Wait!" he managed to shout as another string of spells hit him, one after the other. "Not a d-damn repeating spell!"

The recitation of spells was one of the basic foundations of sorcery—without spoken words, it was impossible to use magic. But a sorcerer in the middle of reciting a spell was vulnerable, sometimes fatally so. Since spells couldn't be abbreviated, one of the first things sorcery researchers tried to discover was a way to speed up the spell recitation process.

The repeating spell was one of those methods. A sorcerer who wanted to cast a repeating spell had to first freeze a recited spell in a state just before activation and then compress that spell deep within the mind. The spell was then tied to a short phrase, so that when the magic was actually needed, only the phrase was necessary.

This allowed a sorcerer to launch a spell rapidly and repeatedly. It was an unorthodox technique that required great mental capacity; an unqualified sorcerer attempting a repeating spell—one unable to handle the overwhelming power of both the spell itself and the Emulator technique—ran the risk of destroying the conscious mind.

Big Shot stared at Raquel in disbelief. "Even among military sorcerers," he blurted, "only one in fifty can do that. How can an amateur—?"

"People of the flames, dance!"

"Aaah!"

"People of the flames, dance!"

"Wait—ow ow ow!"

"People of the flames—"

"I said *wait!*" Big Shot screamed as he struggled to lift his battered body. "You can't do this! It's not fair!"

"Not fair?" Raquel repeated, looking somewhat hurt by the accusation.

Big Shot gritted his teeth as he panted. "You've been toying with me this entire time! Just because you have more mental capacity than me, you think you can show off like this?!"

"I'm not showing off," Raquel replied earnestly. She paused a moment, then clenched both her fists in an impressive display of resolve. "All right—then I'll fight you with *all* my ability, if that's what you want." She nodded, pleased with her decision.

Big Shot realized he'd made a tactical error. "Wh-What? I didn't mean—"

"I'll use a certain-death technique this time. Vaporizing you in one hit is the most serious I can be, so will that do, Mister Murderer?"

"N-No, wait!" Big Shot stammered, but Raquel had already made up her mind.

"Actually," she admitted with a small grin, "I always wanted to try this one." She raised her hand. "Grade 1 military attack technique, Thor!"

Big Shot's desperate screams echoed through the crumbling hallway.

Pacifica gripped the doorframe for support. "That's a c-corpse," she gasped as goosebumps shot up all over her.

It wasn't the body itself that scared her—she'd been to a number of funerals, and she was no stranger to leaving flowers in open caskets.

But the body Sinner held was rotting, its skin so decomposed in parts that the white of bone broke through. It seemed to be a young girl, based on the filthy white blouse and reddish-brown skirt. Her flaxen hair—the only part of her to retain a bit of its original beauty—hung sadly from her shrunken head.

"Who . . . is that?" Pacific whispered.

"What are you afraid of?" Sinner turned to Pacifica, but he didn't look at her. His eyes focused on something far off in the distance.

Pacifica swallowed the bile in her throat. "I'm not afraid," she blurted unconvincingly.

Sinner's eyes moved from whatever he stared at to the body in his arms. "This is my daughter," he murmured. "Lynthia." He brushed a hand lovingly over the corpse's face. "She's sick. To cure her, I need advanced sorcery, and I need money to make that happen. I have no quarrel with you, but you must be sacrificed to save her."

Pacifica went pale. Sinner didn't hold a *sick* child, but one who had obviously died a long time ago. As Sinner's cloudy eyes focused on Pacifica, she suddenly understood.

The man was crazy.

Pacifica tried to keep herself from running back into the comforting, non-insane arms of Big Shot. If Big Shot sounded like a good idea, she was *really* starting to panic.

Maybe you can reason with this Sinner guy, she told herself. *He said he doesn't have anything against you, right?* Hoping beyond hope that it was possible to reason with someone out of his mind, she calmed her voice and took a deep breath.

"Um . . . maybe you should rethink that plan," she said carefully. "I'm sorry, but your daughter has died."

"You lie." Sinner's gloomy voice took on shades of anger. "Lynthia is my daughter. I must protect her. You're lying because you want to take her from me."

Pacifica held out her hands. "I-I just said that—"

"You'll never have her." Sinner gently laid the body on the altar and started toward Pacifica. His eyes bright with madness, he hissed, "I'll kill you first! I'll kill you if you try to touch my baby girl."

He raised an arm and abruptly jerked it down. Something silvery flashed out of his sleeve. Driven by instinct, Pacifica dove to the side.

The silver flash sliced through the air just beside her head, sending a few sheared pieces of hair skyward and hitting her hairclip with a sharp-toned *ping*. The clip clattered to the floor and Pacifica's long hair flowed down onto her shoulders.

Sprawling on the floor, Pacifica stared at the hairclip in amazement. The metal accessory had been severed in half, as if cut with a fine-toothed saw.

A chainlike object had emerged from Sinner's sleeve. Upon closer inspection, it proved to be a string of small, round blades connected with steel wire. Each blade was as wide as a child's hand and had dangerous serrated edges. The weapon flexed like a whip in Sinner's skilled hands.

"This time," he said darkly, "I'll cut more than hair." Sinner jerked back the weapon. As if time were moving in reverse, the whip flew back into the handle Sinner held, and the round blades stacked up like plates. The compacted state of the weapon was small enough for him to conceal it in his clothing.

Pacifica could only stare in disbelief. Her legs, deadened by terror, absolutely refused to move.

I'm going to die, her brain spun. She'd barely avoided Sinner's first attack—the next time he tried, she'd be sliced to pieces. *I'm . . . I'm going to die.*

The fear overwhelmed her, freezing her legs and eliminating any chance of flight. But with that paralysis came a strange sort of calm, a resignation that washed through her mind and deadened her senses.

Fine. Perhaps dying is for the best.

If she died, then Raquel and Shannon wouldn't be in danger—and the world would be spared her poisonous existence.

And yet . . . was she really ready for the end?

The blades of death snaked out again.

In that instant, a thousand conflicting thoughts raced through Pacifica's brain. If she died, the struggle *would* be over—but so would her life as Pacific Casull. She'd never see her friends again; she'd never cook supper with Raquel, or fight with Shannon over chores. She'd be gone, like Father. Nothing more than ash and memories.

Sinner jerked back his arm, the bladed weapon whipping out behind him.

NO! Pacifica didn't want to die—every fiber of her being suddenly begged for life. She choked, as her voice finally ripped out of her throat.

"SHANNON!" she screamed. "HELP!"

From outside the main window, a voice answered, "Hold your horses!"

Shannon, the blue sky behind him, suddenly came crashing through what was left of the stained glass window. Shards of colored glass scattered across the floor as he drew a knife and launched it at Sinner. The deadly blade whipped through the air.

Caught off guard, Sinner narrowly avoided the knife. His string of blades whipped back to smash harmlessly into a wall behind him.

Shannon flew over Sinner's head and landed in front of Pacifica. A rope swayed back and forth just outside the shattered window, testament to Shannon's daring rappel from the roof. He quickly turned to Sinner, leaving his little sister to stare at his back.

"Sh-Shannon?" Pacifica breathed, her eyes wide with disbelief. He'd actually heard her?

Shannon sighed, his eyes locked on his opponent. "A simple 'thank you' would be fine," he muttered. "Although

I'll also accept, 'That was the most fantastic entrance I've ever seen.' "

Pacifica was so glad to hear Shannon complaining that she almost broke down into sobs. Resisting the urge to cling to him, she took a few deep breaths, then shakily pushed herself to her feet. "Wh-What took you so long?" she asked, sounding indignant. "Because of you, my hairclip's ruined."

"Yeah, yeah. I got here as fast as I could."

"That's fast? You didn't have to climb the roof."

He snorted. "Then the next time I rescue *Her Highness*," he snapped, "I'll walk up to the front door and knock!"

Pacifica was glad that Shannon had his back to her. That way, he couldn't see the tears welling up in her eyes. He hadn't abandoned her. And if Shannon had come, Pacifica guessed that Raquel was elsewhere, taking care of Big Shot. Her brother and sister still wanted her.

I don't have to die, she thought. *I'm Pacifica Casull, and I can stay Pacifica Casull. It's okay to live . . . right?*

Of course, there was no answer to that question— but as she watched Shannon draw his blade to protect her, she couldn't help but feel substantially better.

"Gosh, Mister Hit Man, you should see the look on your face."

Big Shot stumbled down the hallway, hotly pursued by Raquel's Thor spell. Thor was a semi-autonomous Class 1 military pursuit spell that automatically followed whatever target was programmed into it. Raquel smiled, pleased that her spell had worked properly, and watched Big Shot as he floundered away in panic.

The Thor spell was designed to take the shape of a humanoid giant, twice a normal man's height and covered in rippling muscles. The human appearance was only for show, since Thor was actually made up of lightning manipulated by sorcery. Upon contact with its target, Thor could emit an electrical force equivalent to dozens of lightning bolts

Raquel had mildly altered the spell from its original design: the electric giant skipped after Big Shot like a pleased puppy. The sight of the muscular warrior grinning broadly as it hopped was enough to make anyone doubt his own sanity.

"I thought his pursuit speed would be a little faster," Raquel mused, "but I'm sure he'll catch up soon enough. Plus, he's so *cute!*"

Big Shot couldn't be bothered by the ridiculous display—he was too busy trying not to die. He might be a powerful wizard, but he wasn't exactly athletic.

"Still," Raquel commented, touching her chin with a finger. "I guess I should adjust the semi-autonomous pursuit routine. Huh, Mister Hired Killer?"

❧

Sinner's sword sliced down from above Shannon's head. Faster than his opponent, Shannon arced his own blade up and easily met Sinner's thrust.

Yet the instant he blocked, Sinner's sword segmented beyond the point where it contacted with Shannon's weapon and whipped up for the back of Shannon's head. Shannon heaved hard against the still-solid part of Sinner's sword and ducked. The flying blades wrapped around empty air instead of around Shannon's neck.

He and Sinner leapt apart. Shannon's eyes followed the blade whip as Sinner yanked it back into its solid form.

"So he's got a Dark Sword," Shannon muttered as he absently rubbed a cut on his cheek. He'd avoided most of the blow, but not the tip; without his hardened leather armor, his right shoulder would have been sliced open.

Unlike ordinary swords, a Dark Sword was a weapon customized for non-traditional fighting. Dark Swords were found mainly in the hands of mercenaries from rural provinces and existed in nearly infinite varieties. To someone trained only to fight against traditional swordsmanship, a Dark Sword could be unpredictable and deadly—the very reason they were created in the first place.

Since Dark Swords were generally used to catch an opponent off guard, their weakness was that once their trickery was unmasked, it reduced their effectiveness. Unfortunately, Shannon could see that Sinner was fully aware of his weapon's advantages and drawbacks, and that losing the element of surprise wasn't going to hold the man back much.

Great, Shannon thought bitterly. Shannon's own sword was so rare that it could have been considered a type of Dark Sword, but Sinner had the definite advantage with his extended reach. At least when Sinner's weapon was fully extended, he was left vulnerable—that was when Shannon needed to strike. The only question was whether or not Shannon could get within range and still manage to keep his limbs.

"Who the hell are you, anyway?" Shannon called across the chapel.

"You want to hurt Lynthia." Sinner's voice was stone.
"Who?"

"You want to take Lynthia from me, but I won't let you. I won't *let* you."

The extended Dark Sword whipped sideways. Shannon jumped out of the swinging weapon's path, but the tip of the blade bounced off the floor and came at him from another direction. Shannon barely managed to avoid being beheaded. As he jerked away, the weapon skimmed the side of his head, taking a bit of his scalp with it. He quickly retreated.

Pacifica ran to his side. "Shannon!" she cried.

"Stay back." He glanced at her from the corner of his eye. "Is that a corpse on the altar?"

"She was his daughter—I think she died of some disease. But the guy's crazy, Shannon! He thinks she's still alive!"

Shannon could already tell from Sinner's eyes that there was something seriously wrong with the man. The way Sinner stood in front of that corpse with his sword ready left little room for speculation: Shannon didn't doubt that Sinner honestly wanted to protect the girl.

⚙⚙

"Shannon?" Pacifica asked quickly. "Do you think you can beat him?"

"If you go and hide until it's over. I can't protect you and fight him at the same time."

He heard Pacifica start to protest. "I can't just—"

"Leave me? Sure you can."

Pacifica stomped a foot in frustration. She hesitated another moment, then turned and fled the chapel.

Sinner remained still, so Shannon just stared at him until he was sure Pacifica had gone.

"Now," he said evenly as he shifted his feet. "You've got my full attention, so let's try this again."

In response, Sinner rushed forward with his compacted Dark Sword; Shannon ran to meet him. When Sinner slashed at Shannon from the side, Shannon twisted his body and swung his own weapon. A painful metallic clang echoed throughout the chapel. As before, the Dark Sword segmented and bent wildly at the point of impact.

Perfect, Shannon thought. He swung his sword in a large arc. The Dark Sword changed directions just before striking him and instead wound around and around Shannon's blade before coming to a stop.

Sinner's thin eyebrows shot up. "What?" he barked, but it was already too late.

Shannon plunged his blade down to pin it (and thus Sinner's weapon) into the floor. Shannon clenched both fists, causing the metal rods in his leather gloves to bulge up, and swung back for a final punch.

Sinner just smiled. He lithely whipped down his left arm and released another Dark Sword from its sleeve.

Shannon tried to rear back, but couldn't overcome his own momentum. His metal-reinforced fist slammed into the new blade; the Dark Sword burst into a whip and wrapped itself around his arm and up his shoulder.

"First," Sinner said darkly, "I'll take an arm."

To allow freedom of movement, only a small percentage of Shannon's arms were covered with armor.

Whether Sinner ripped off the entire limb or just slashed it to ribbons, Shannon had a bad feeling he was going to bleed to death.

Sinner sneered. "A good assassin is always ambidextrous. You're good, but you're inexperienced."

"I'll remember that for next time," Shannon muttered as he carefully slid his free hand to his waist. He slipped his index finger into a small metal ring and jerked. His right shoulder guard flipped up, exposing a small cylinder aimed right at Sinner.

Sinner gave a start. "What the—?"

He tried to pull in his Dark Sword, but Shannon shoved up against him and pinned the segmented weapon between them. With a pop, a small dart fired from the cylinder and plunged into Sinner's shoulder.

Sinner grunted and loosened his grip. Shannon took the opportunity to clench his free fist and slam it onto Sinner's fingers, causing the second Dark Sword to hit the floor with a clang. The sword slithered off of Shannon's arm as he stepped back.

"Here's some advice for *you*," Shannon offered as he shook his numb arm. "When you've got the upper hand, don't lose it by giving a lecture."

Sinner looked at his own shoulder, then at Shannon's armor. "A hidden weapon," he murmured, as if that fact weren't obvious.

"Yeah, this armor is full of good stuff. Spring-loaded darts and the like."

The dart was only powerful enough for a point-blank surprise attack, but sometimes that was all it took to turn the tables on an opponent. Such tricks were never employed by traditional swordsmen, who only believed in crossing blades; darts were more the fare of reconnaissance troops, Special Forces, and mercenaries trained in multiple weapons and concerned with survival above all else.

Sinner yanked the barbed dart from his shoulder. A thin stream of scarlet blood spilled out.

Shannon took another step back. "I'm not usually one to pull that sort of thing," he explained, "but I don't have time to worry about formality right now. This is your chance to back off—it's not worth risking your life over this if your daughter's already dead."

Ferocious anger visibly welled up inside the haggard man. His crazed eyes burned with a new fury; his fingertips twitched by his sides.

Shannon felt the hair stand up on the back of his neck.

Sinner screamed and charged at Shannon with nothing more than his fingernails. Shannon easily dodged, so Sinner spun to the sword embedded in the floor and ripped the tightly coiled Dark Sword off of Shannon's blade.

His hands bloody, he dragged the chainlike weapon across the floor as he turned back to Shannon. "Yaaaa!"

Sinner remained glued to the floor as he wailed at the top of his lungs. Shannon listened to the sound reverberate through the chapel and wondered whether it was a battle cry or a cry of anguish. Unless it was a prayer?

"That's right!" Shannon yelled. "Your daughter's dead! Nothing you can do will change that!" The words were hard for him to say—he didn't enjoy dragging a crazy man back to the thing that had made him snap—but Shannon wanted to at least try to reason his way out of the fight. He somehow doubted that was going to happen.

Sinner let out another shriek, then charged straight for Shannon. The older man frantically swung his sword without any semblance of his former strategy. Shannon easily avoided the attacks.

"Why are you doing this?" he asked as he dodged Sinner's whips. "You're soiling her memory with your own cowardice. Give her a proper burial and stop defiling her body!"

"SILENCE!" Sinner screamed at the top of his lungs.

With a maddened cry, he lifted his sword over his head and swung it down on Shannon. Shannon slipped to the side and let the Dark Sword race down to the altar. Unfortunately, both he and Sinner had been too late to realize the consequences.

The fully extended blade came down onto the little body resting there. Bits of mummified flesh flew into the air as, with a soft crunch, the corpse of the young girl split in half with heartbreaking ease.

A hellish silence fell over the room. Sinner, his face as white as a ghost's, dropped the handle of his blade. The Dark Sword clattered to the ground.

"No . . ." Sinner breathed. "NO!" Shaking crazily, he staggered away from the corpse as if he were in a trance.

When he looked down at his bloody hands, his wide eyes filled with unbridled fear.

Sinner's face contorted into a twisted image of guilt and panic. He stumbled back toward his daughter's body, so oblivious to Shannon that he physically brushed past the younger man.

"My Lynthia," Sinner mumbled as he knelt down by the corpse. "I'm so sorry, my precious Lynthia . . . will you forgive me? Here, let's take care of that."

Sinner gently pushed the two halves of the body together. Shannon looked away and tried not to be sick.

"There, that's better. See? You're all better now, Lynthia. Open your eyes, my sweet."

Dark, empty sockets were all that stared back at Sinner. He murmured more promises of love as he brushed back the corpse's hair, but then, as if confused, he stopped.

"Th-That's strange," he whispered. "You don't have any eyes, Lynthia. How long have you not had any . . . ?"

Sinner shakily got to his feet, realization dawning in his eyes. "How could I have missed that?" he asked no one. "Your . . . your sweet eyes are gone. Where did they . . . ?"

a tomb for the Lost princess

Shannon didn't want to watch, but he turned back when he heard Sinner drag his blade up from the floor. The older man stacked the Dark Sword with shaking hands and pointed the tip at his neck.

"Oh, Lynthia!" Sinner cried as he threw back his head. "Forgive me!"

Closing his eyes, Sinner plunged the Dark Sword into his throat. The tip of the sword pushed through the back of his neck with a gory squelching sound.

Shannon's mouth opened, but no sound came out. He watched as Sinner crumpled to the floor, twitched several times, then finally went still. A dark pool of blood leaked from under the assassin and soaked his dingy cloak scarlet.

Shannon swallowed. "I'm . . . sure she forgives you," he whispered, his eyebrows furrowing. It wasn't much, but he couldn't think of anything else to say.

Shannon slowly retrieved his sword. *What am I doing?* he wondered as he glanced back at Sinner's body. The man had lost his mind over his daughter's death—rather than accept his loss, he'd dragged out her last living moments and ruined his life. And yet . . . Shannon couldn't help but feel like he might be doing

135

the same thing. He was trying to protect a girl who was prophesized to destroy the world.

Am I just as crazy? he thought as he slid his sword into its sheath. *Am I going to ruin my life and die like him?*

Shannon let out a shaky breath. He dragged Sinner's body over to Lynthia's so the two could lie together. As the young warrior straightened again, he made a conscious decision to avoid Sinner's fate. Whatever the future held, he would never let love drive him away from reality.

He sighed. *Not if I can help it*, he added silently, his shoulders slumping with the thought.

❧

"If you're going to kill me," Big Shot panted from his position on the floor, "then just kill me! I've had enough of this!"

In response, the electric giant skipped cheerfully toward the killer. Big Shot closed his eyes and braced himself.

The giant suddenly tripped over a loose brick. Hitting the floor with a thud, a few small electrical discharges fizzled in the air before the Thor apparition vanished into nothing.

"Whoops," Raquel said, raising a hand to her mouth.

Big Shot was stupefied. "A . . . a dud?" he croaked, his beady eyes wide. His gaze flew to Raquel, but she only looked away.

"That's strange," she mumbled. "I wonder why?"

A normal Thor apparition would use only a tiny part of its power to destroy an insignificant brick. It would never trip over something so small, nor discharge all of its destructive power and disappear before reaching its target. Big Shot glared daggers at Raquel as he stood. "You!" he snarled. "You . . . you NUTCASE!"

Startled, Raquel took a step back. "People make mistakes."

"You gave me quite a workout," Big Shot spat out with a half-crazed grimace. "Do you always test your spells out on your worthy opponents?"

"Well, look at it this way: you probably lost some weight." Raquel smiled nervously.

Big Shot held out his palms. "That's it!" he roared. "Prepare to die!"

A loud clunk cut him off, and Big Shot pitched forward. He hit the floor with his mouth agape, his fingertips twitching and his eyes rolled back.

2

Behind him, holding a brick in one hand, stood Pacifica.

"Pacifica!" Raquel exclaimed, pressing her palms together in gratitude. "You came to rescue me!"

Pacifica gave her an exasperated look. "Rescue *you?*" she repeated. "I thought you and Shannon were here to rescue *me!*"

"Well, if you want to get technical about it."

With a disgusted look on her face, Pacifica threw the brick at the unconscious Big Shot; it struck the portly killer directly in the stomach. He emitted a faint croaking sound but otherwise didn't stir, so the two girls paid him no more attention.

"Have you seen Shannon?" Raquel asked.

Pacifica nodded quickly, gripping her sister's arm. "He was fighting the other guy—the really creepy one. Raquel, you have to go help him! We have to do something!"

"I don't think we have to worry about that," Raquel commented as she looked over Pacifica's head.

Pacifica turned. Shannon emerged from the depths of the dark hallway, his steps slow and his eyelids droopy.

"Shannon!" they both called.

He waved unenthusiastically, thus proving he was fine.

෴

Something tapped Miyutia's bedroom window lightly.

The girl stirred in her bed, intending to turn right over and go back to sleep. She was just about to drift off when the sound occurred again, then a third time. She sat up in bed and groggily rubbed her eyes.

"What's that?" she mumbled. Miyutia stalked over to her shutters and opened them. Tiny snowflakes drifted down from the night sky; it was the year's first snowfall.

She stuck her head out of the window for a better look at the pretty view of Manurhin blanketed in white.

"Wow," she murmured.

She looked down to see a familiar face. "Pacifica?"

"Hey," Pacifica answered with a shy wave. "Sorry for bothering you in the middle of the night."

"That's . . . okay. What's wrong?"

"I wanted to ask you something." Pacifica cleared her throat. "Do you remember what I said in class, Miyutia? About what you'd do if I wasn't really Pacifica Casull?"

She swallowed. "I just want to, um, know—if that was true, would you still be my friend?"

"What kind of stup—" Miyutia stopped herself mid-sentence when she saw the look on Pacifica's face. After a moment's pause, she started over. "Uh, I guess so. If your name was different, you'd still be you. If you grew up somewhere else as a completely different person, and if the two of us met, I'm sure we'd be friends."

"Really?" Pacifica's face brightened.

Miyutia sighed. "Look, Pacifica. I don't know what this is all about, but you'll catch a cold if you stay out there. I'll go open the front door."

"N-No," Pacifica said quickly. "That's okay—I have to go."

"Oh. All right." Miyutia waved. "Good night."

"Good night," Pacifica said, forcing herself to smile.

"I'll see you on Sunday," Miyutia added.

When Pacifica didn't answer, Miyutia assumed that her friend hadn't heard her. Leaning sleepily against her windowsill, Miyutia watched as Pacifica disappeared, her slight body lost behind a white curtain of gently falling snow.

a tomb for the Lost princess

The snow accumulated slowly, symbolic of the long winter ahead. Everything fell under that veneer of white—everything, good and bad.

Shannon watched from the city gate as the layer of white blanketed the familiar landmarks of his home.

Nearby, Raquel bowed to Finebell. The duke's bodyguard had brought a carriage and planned to see the Casulls off.

The carriage was small, unadorned, and painted completely black. It was a standard passenger wagon, drawn by four horses.

The vehicle consisted of a small cabin, a driver's seat, and a separate luggage compartment. It also housed some considerable military extras, unseen to the casual observer.

"Thank you so much for everything," Raquel said, bowing to Finebell once again.

"I'm only following orders." The only thing that belied Fineball's chilly attitude was the live chicken she held protectively against her chest—Desert Eagle, whose feathers were puffed up against the nighttime cold.

"Why didn't Duke Franki come?" Raquel asked.

"He may not look it, but His Grace is quite sentimental. He strongly dislikes saying goodbye." Finebell shrugged. "You probably haven't noticed, but to a childless man like him, you make him feel a parent."

"Right," Shannon muttered. "What parent kicks his own kids out of town?"

"Shannon!"

Fineball shot him a look. "It seems His Grace isn't the only one who hates goodbyes."

Shannon ignored her.

"But I'm not just talking about you," she continued. "To him, *all* of the townspeople are his children. It's for the sake of the others that he asked you to leave. Can you understand that?"

Shannon nodded and glanced down at the fowl that Finebell held against her chest. "Are you really going to keep that bird?"

"Why not? She's sweet." Finebell gently petted the chicken. The fearsome Desert Eagle seemed strangely calm in Finebell's arms.

"To each his own. But I wouldn't go near her eggs without a—"

"She's back," Raquel interrupted.

Shannon and Finebell looked up to see Pacifica walk through the city gate. Her eyes were fixed on the ground, and an invisible sadness rounded out the usual square of her shoulders.

Shannon eyed her carefully. "Did you do what you wanted to do?" he asked, his tone more inquisitive than the words.

She looked up with a small smile. "Mm," she replied. "Thanks."

Ignoring the snow on the ground, Finebell knelt before Pacifica. "Your Highness," she said.

Pacifica shook her head. "Just call me Pacifica, please."

"Very well, Pacifica. I bear a message from the duke." She cleared her throat. " 'Do not think yourself unfortunate, for you have something others only dream of. Treasure what you have, and don't be ashamed to feel pride.' "

Pacifica wrinkled her face. "Uh . . . okay?"

"You'll understand some day."

Pacifica looked to the chicken in Finebell's arms. "Well, Desert Eagle, I guess this is goodbye."

The chicken jumped into the air and fluttered to the ground with a cluck. The bird lowered itself for a moment, then stood and stepped aside. A single white egg lay in a depression in the snow.

Pacifica and Finebell looked at each other. Surely the chicken didn't understand what was going on?

"Desert Eagle," Pacifica breathed as she picked up the egg. "Is this a going-away present?"

"All right," Shannon said impatiently. "Let's *go.*"

Pacifica climbed into the cabin, and Raquel took her place on the driver's bench next to Shannon. With a light crack of the whip, the horses began to trot.

Finebell and Desert Eagle watched the carriage pass by. Without glancing back, Shannon made a last request of Finebell. "Tell the duke we're grateful."

She nodded. "I will," she murmured as the carriage rattled through the gate.

With that, Shannon, Raquel, and Pacifica left their peaceful lives behind them, and set out into the unknown.

THE WEARY PROTECTOR

Shannon let out a long, annoyed sigh. *What a hassle.* He would have said that aloud, but even that would have been a hassle.

He'd tied his long black hair back into a simple ponytail and wore a long black cloak around his lithe body. Not because he was in mourning, and not because he was planning nighttime espionage, but because he didn't want to make getting dressed in the morning more complicated than it had to be. He looked very dashing.

In certain circles he was known as Shannon Casull, the Guardian. It was a name spoken with reverence and fear.

In the year that had passed since leaving home, Shannon had earned his nickname by defeating the many assassins dispatched by the palace. Each time he and Raquel emerged victorious with their lives, their skill levels increased and their bravery grew.

Today, like many other days, he fought off a new group of attackers. But the assassin who was locked in a life-and-death battle with Shannon found the bored look on Shannon's face highly demoralizing.

"Wh-What kind of man *are* you?" the assassin demanded.

Shannon snorted. "A man who missed his nap today."

They fought on a side trail just off the main road. The maddeningly straight trail was crowded on both sides by thick brush—nobody in his right mind would travel that path after dusk, as it was the perfect place to end up ambushed. The two blades that crashed together reflected the sky's dimming orange twilight.

"All right," Shannon snapped. "I've had it with this." He flicked his sword, knocking his opponent's massive broadsword to the ground. The assassin instinctively turned to run for his weapon, but froze when Shannon's blade pressed against the side of his neck.

Perhaps Shannon's light, saber-like blade had an advantage over the clunky broadsword, but more than that, Shannon was fast. *Very* fast—and accurate.

The bearded opponent trembled as Shannon's blade grazed alongside his throat. Swallowing carefully, the assassin still managed an indignant scowl.

"You conceited brat," he spat out. "Don't you realize what you're doing? Even an uneducated peasant boy should know about the Oracle of Saint Grendel!"

Shannon ignored the comment. "Look," he said darkly. "You came to kill a little girl, right? If you've come to kill, you'd better know the stakes."

In contrast to Shannon's worn-in, scuffed leather armor, the bearded man wore a clean set that had probably never seen a fight. His swordsmanship had been by the book, with movements clearly memorized long ago at fencing school. The man was no mercenary.

"Fool!" the assassin snapped. "You're making a terrible—"

He stopped in mid-sentence as a red rivulet leaked onto Shannon's blade. The man shot a panicked look around him. The other three members of his team lay on the ground nearby, two in hardened leather armor and the third in the embroidered blue robe of a sorcerer. When calculating the fighting strength of a unit, a sorcerer trained in attack spells was usually considered equivalent to ten soldiers.

Shannon had defeated them all.

The chests of the fallen men still moved with their breathing, so they obviously weren't dead. Disabling multiple opponents without killing them—a feat that required unbelievable skill—only went to prove how dangerous Shannon was.

"What do you want to lose?" Shannon asked. "Your eyesight, your kneecaps, or your sword arm? Take your pick."

"Listen to me! Don't you realize that the girl—"

"All right; I'll choose for you."

"Wait!" the bearded man suddenly blurted out. The indignant expression on his face vanished when Shannon raised his sword.

Shannon paused. He raised an eyebrow.

The assassin swallowed hard, sending a few more droplets of his blood down his throat. "Surely you know of the Oracle of Saint Grendel from fifteen years ago?"

"No." He shrugged.

The bearded man's jaw dropped.

"Never heard . . . how could you not know of the prophecy?! Listen, that girl—"

"You already tried that one," Shannon said as he raised his sword once more.

"No, wait!" Panic flashed across the bearded man's face. Then, suddenly, his expression shifted from one of fear to one of relief. He broke out laughing.

"Ha ha ha!" he guffawed. "Now we've got you, you stupid brat!"

Shannon lowered his sword. He wondered if perhaps the man had lost his mind, but then recognized the look in the assassin's eyes—the arrogant glimmer of one convinced of victory.

"Now what?" Shannon muttered.

"Look behind you!" With a large (albeit still shaky) grin, the bearded man pointed to the area behind Shannon. Shannon scowled and turned.

The bearded man took advantage of the opportunity and quickly moved to attack Shannon from behind . . . until he froze. Something—his own survival instinct, perhaps—sensed a dangerous new emotion in Shannon, and he stopped cold.

A fiery, murderous rage radiated off of Shannon in waves. Knowing better than to provoke that, the bearded man shrunk back.

The Casull family's carriage hadn't changed much since the day they'd received it: despite the simple design of the wagon, inside it lay devices and gadgets that had saved Shannon and his sisters from harm many times. From the steel-reinforced shutters to the fire-resistant paint, to the armor-disguised-as-blankets on the horses, everything about the coach was military grade.

Raquel, standing beside the carriage and wearing the same black cloak and leather gloves as Shannon, looked even more like her brother when she matched him in garb. Beside her stood Pacifica, slightly taller than before, dressed in a unique combination of leather and fabric, and sporting a look of great distaste upon her face. Between the two girls stood a man dressed as a villager, whose most distinguishing characteristic was his lack of distinguishing characteristics—which was exactly why the daggers he held against each of the girls' throats looked so out of place.

"Raquel," Shannon said darkly.

"Huh?" came Raquel's lazy reply.

"Nice job over there."

"Throw down your sword," the man called. Shannon could tell the words were no mere threat; the man had the emotionless voice of a calm professional for whom killing had become routine. Shannon sighed.

"Whatever," he muttered as he stabbed his sword into the ground and took three steps back.

"No!" Pacifica shrieked, her desire to scream unhindered by the blade against her neck. "What are you *doing*, you moron?!"

Shannon rolled his eyes. *Here it comes.*

"This is so like you, Shannon! As soon as you start fighting, you forget all about guarding us. Now look at the mess we're in!" Pacifica glared daggers at her older brother, the blue of her irises glittering with fury. "Then you have the nerve to act like it's all such a big hassle! If everything annoys you so darn much, then stop breathing—you won't have *any* hassles to worry about anymore!"

"Pacifica," Shannon snapped. "I mean, *Your Highness*, we took this dangerous shortcut because you whined about how much you wanted to sleep indoors tonight."

"And?" Pacifica clearly didn't make the connection.

"And if *Her Highness* would consider her situation more carefully once in a blue moon, then her humble guards could protect her more effectively."

"Silence! It's too late for feigned subservience now— not after your long-standing arrogance!" She crossed her arms. "I should have you thrown in a dungeon, but I'm basically a nice person, so I'll give you another chance. You have until the count of ten to write a short essay on how sorry you are."

Shannon glared at her. Pacifica kept her gaze locked with his for a few moments, then, finally, she dropped her eyes to the ground. Her lips curled in a frown.

"Come again?" Shannon asked pointedly.

"Help," Pacifica murmured.

Shannon shifted his gaze to Raquel, who'd watched the entire exchange with casual interest. "Give me a hand?" he asked.

Raquel raised one hand; her movement was so relaxed that the man with the dagger didn't react at all. She pointed her long, pale fingers at the knife by her throat.

"Thunder Hammer, strike!" Crackling purple arcs of electricity shot from the space just in front of Raquel's fingertips, piercing through the dagger and into the assassin. The man dropped like a stone. He quivered on the ground, his mouth open in shock and his hair standing on end.

Although he did lose the use of his legs for some time, the man was actually quite lucky—the real Mjolnir spell, a military attack spell used by Linevan royal troops, was strong enough to cause instant death. Raquel had reconstructed the top-secret spell from her mother's notes and used her considerable skill to keep it from being lethal.

The bearded opponent's eyes almost popped out of his head. "No," he croaked. "That's im-im-impos . . ."

"Impossible?" Shannon smirked without humor. "Is that what you're trying to say?"

Raquel smiled. "Actually," she said, as if happy to explain, "I used the repeating spell technique. You compress the activation procedure for one spell in an Emulator—which is separate from your own self—then you later recite a short spell that expands and triggers the main spell. The technique even lets someone who isn't a sorcerer temporarily—"

"Raquel," Shannon interrupted, "I'm pretty sure that's enough."

Raquel frowned at her brother. Shannon ignored her and went to pull his sword out of the ground.

"All right," he said, turning back to the now-pale assassin. "Did you take that extra time to decide which body part you need the least?"

The man could only stare at the gleaming blade, his eyes wide with fear.

❧❦

The coach continued down the narrow side road in near darkness, finally free of assassins. Raquel sat in the driver's seat with Shannon by her side, her eyes on the faint lights of a town that flickered in the distance. It looked so deceptively peaceful.

Pacifica opened the cabin window and stuck her head out. "Shannon," she piped up. "How much longer?"

"Can't you see the town up ahead?" Shannon gestured to the lights. "We're almost there."

Pacifica reached out of the window, grabbed Shannon's ear, and tugged it to her lips.

"You *always* say that!" she shrieked. "And you never mean it!"

"Let go!" Shannon shouted back. "And be quiet, would you?!" He grabbed the back of her neck with one hand and pinched her lips together with the other.

"So," he asked through gritted teeth. "Any more demands, princess?"

"Shtop!" Pacifica flailed her arms. "Mmmgph! Mmgph!"

"I don't understand—you should learn to enunciate."

Raquel frowned. "I want to play," she said with a hint of envy.

Shannon gestured to his captive sister. "Give me a free hand and I'll get you in on this."

Pacifica decided to fight back. She stuck her finger in Shannon's mouth and pulled.

"Rrraangph!" Shannon protested. He and Pacifica glared at each other, neither of them letting the other go.

"Germs," Raquel calmly reminded them. "Your hands are filthy."

Shannon spat out Pacifica's finger and pushed her head back into the wagon. "All right," he ordered. "That's enough!" He rubbed his cheek with a hand. "My face will end up all stretched out."

"Ha!" Pacifica mocked as she defiantly poked her head out again. Her lips had swollen a bit, her own war wound. "You'll look like someone with premature-aging-lazy-face-itis. Instead of just *acting* like an old man, you'll look like one, too! Old man Shannon! Old man Shannon!"

"Stop making up disease names."

Raquel slowed down the carriage, tugging at Shannon's sleeve as she did so. "Look," she said as she pointed up the road.

In the middle of the path stood a lone boy. He seemed to be in his mid-teens, and wore a long cloak that covered him from neck to ankles. Raquel pulled on the reins and brought the coach to a stop. The boy walked over to them.

"Sorry for the inconvenience," he said, tilting his young face upward. "But I need your help."

Pacifica peeked out of the carriage. The boy had soft chestnut hair and a dignified, almost aristocratic air. She noticed right away that he was also quite handsome.

Getting a closer look at Shannon and Pacifica, the boy turned to Raquel. "Are they sick?" he asked. "Their faces are swollen."

"No!" shouted Pacifica.

"They were just showing affection," Raquel stated, her face the picture of perfect innocence.

"Oh." He raised his eyebrows suggestively. "Hot."

"NO!" Pacifica shouted even louder. "EW!" She made an exaggerated gagging motion, obnoxious enough to successfully bother everyone.

Despite the boy's friendly banter, Shannon still found him suspicious. "What do you want?" Shannon asked brusquely.

The boy smiled. "Not much," he said as he walked to Shannon's side of the carriage. "I'd just like you to die."

A clash of swords erupted in the night air.

Shannon and the boy pushed on their locked weapons, the metal scraping together loudly.

Both had drawn in a blur—Shannon, his father's sword; the boy, a beautiful battleaxe. They each possessed blades of extraordinary craftmanship.

A battleaxe was a devastating weapon in skilled hands. Not only did it land a massive blow when the wielder took advantage of the blade's centrifugal force, but it could be used with as much precision as a sword— if the wielder was properly trained.

The handle of the boy's axe had actually been folded under his cloak; he'd deployed it in one smooth motion, using the momentum of his swing to unfold the axe to its full length. Not only did his movements speak to the amount of time he put into training, his deft handling of his weapon lacked the stiffness common to those with little combat experience. There was no doubt about it: the boy was an expert.

"Pacifica!" Shannon shouted. "Stay inside!" The alarm in his voice was clear, so Pacifica did as she was told. Raquel jumped off the coach in order to stay out of her brother's way.

Shannon threw his weight against his opponent's weapon. Rather than resisting, the boy stepped back to parry Shannon's strike. Shannon used the opportunity to jump down from his restrictive position on the carriage.

"Not bad," the boy remarked, his smile never leaving his face. "You sensed that I was an enemy before I even attacked."

"Of course I did," Shannon said flatly. "You were *too* pleasant."

The boy chuckled. "Is that right?"

"Who are you?"

"Tactician Christopher Armalite. I'm with the Royal Special Forces Battalion Five, also known as Adamant Arrow. You can call me Chris."

Chris looked like a perfectly ordinary boy—save for his eyes. They were clear, ice blue, and very, very piercing.

Shannon felt a chill run down his spine. *This one's a cold-blooded killer.*

"I almost forgot," the boy said, ignoring Shannon's seething glare. "Before I kill you, I wanted to ask if you met up with a group led by a bearded man."

"You're with *them?*"

"Technically, no. I was ordered to work with them, but they set out before I got to the rendezvous point."

Shannon spat. "When I left them," he replied darkly, "they were lying at the side of the road with their newly-broken bones. You're telling me you care?"

"About those stupid, decrepit knights? No. There's no point in living after losing a battle."

First knights, then a tactician in the Royal Special Forces. The news worried Shannon; it meant the palace had given up on hired killers and was finally sending its own troops. Mercenaries had no official ties and therefore wouldn't incriminate the palace, but if royal troops were on their way, it meant the palace was desperate enough to stop caring about accountability.

The palace was most likely eager to eliminate the Casull siblings before word of the Scrapped Princess leaked out. Not only did it mean an increased number of organized men against Pacifica, but the palace had several elite troops at their disposal—such as the unmatched Anvar Knights and several Special Forces units. Shannon wasn't exactly sure how skilled the Special Forces were, but if the boy in front of him was any indication, they were at least as good as the rumors claimed.

"Although," Chris added after a moment, "it would've been easier for me if you *had* killed them."

"It would've been easier for me, too," Shannon snapped. "So are you going to fight or not?"

"Actually, I think I'm going to have to call it quits. I should check up on the knights—my superiors would give me hell if I didn't and something happened to them."

Without waiting for a reply, Chris jumped backward, folding his axe with a flick of his arm. By the time he'd landed, the axe had already disappeared back inside his long cloak.

He turned to leave, then suddenly looked back.

"One last thing," he said. "Why are you protecting the girl?"

Shannon and Raquel glanced back at the coach. They couldn't see Pacifica, but they were sure she could hear them.

"You know about the prophecy, don't you?" Chris twirled his fingers in the air. "She'll be the cause of calamity. Piles of corpses, rivers of blood . . . What do you gain by protecting someone whom everyone would be happy to see dead?"

Chris stopped talking just in time to catch the knife thrown at his face. Shannon hadn't aimed to kill, but he'd still launched it with all the force of his anger.

The boy playfully tossed the knife in a high arc behind him. The weapon spun around and around before vanishing into the darkness.

"Why are you so angry? You must be used to hearing that by now."

Shannon glared and lowered his throwing arm. It didn't matter how often people said it—it still hurt every time.

Chris shrugged. "So be it," he said with an enigmatic smile. He turned on his heels and walked away.

Raquel held up her hands for an attack spell, but quickly decided against it. Not only was it cowardly, but Chris could probably avoid it.

Shannon sighed as he and his sister watched Chris disappear. "I guess they're sending out the *real* fighters now," he murmured.

Raquel nodded silently.

❧

The siblings didn't stay at an inn that night. They couldn't get permission to enter the town armed, and Shannon refused to waltz in without a weapon when Special Forces troops could be lurking around. Instead, the three of them decided to camp on the town's outskirts—a decision that predictably drew more whining from Pacifica.

"I can't *believe* we're stuck outside again," the girl moaned as she unrolled her sleeping bag. She gave the bedroll a swift kick to drive her point home.

Raquel's voice drifted over from behind the coach. "Supper will be ready in a minute, you two."

Shannon's lips twisted. He knew that Raquel's cooking had a one-in-three chance of coming out a complete disaster . . . not because she was a bad cook, but because she always tried to use sorcery in her cooking.

"I hope it came out okay," Raquel wondered aloud, doing nothing to ease his fears.

"We'll see," Shannon murmured.

He took some comfort in the thought that Raquel already had an Asgard sensor spell deployed, and thus probably had no energy to use magic on the food. Once cast, Asgard lasted a full day and alerted its creator if anyone tried to approach. It normally took at least three sorcerers to cast the Asgard sensor—three sorcerers, or one very talented Raquel.

Remembering why she had needed to cast the spell in the first place, Shannon picked up his sword and lurched to his feet. Spell or no, sorcery wasn't infallible; he still wanted to take a look around before supper.

It was quiet around the campsite. Shannon, tired from the events of the day, was thankful for the respite. He rested his sheathed sword on his shoulder as he walked.

Sorcery, he thought with mild interest. *I remember studying sorcery.*

As a sorcerer, Shannon had an abundance of magical power—more than his sister did, his mother had told him. But sorcery wasn't about power. Rather than generating energy, sorcerers merely manipulated the hidden rules that ran the tangible world in order to cause particular outcomes. The process was analogous to placing one's hand in a river to affect the flow.

Technically speaking, the term "magical power" referred to a person's mental capacity for invoking a spell. A greater mental capacity allowed a sorcerer to better invoke complicated, powerful spells or multiple spells simultaneously.

Among sorcerers, it was universally accepted that mental capacity was fixed at birth and couldn't be increased with training or practice, although nobody was quite certain whether capacity was something inherited from parents, or gained at birth by chance.

If mental capacity was a measure of sorcery talent, then Shannon had it in spades. What he lacked was the ability to *control* that—he didn't have the instinct or intuition for invoking a spell in his mind and moderating its generation and effect.

Simply put, he lacked the skill needed to make use of his considerable talent. Shannon rubbed his eyes.

Whatever, he thought. *So Father made me the swordsman, and Mother made Raquel the sorcerer.*

Raquel had started mimicking her mother and invoking spells by age three; she clearly had enough skill for both of them.

Shannon suddenly stopped, his boots kicking up a small cloud of dust around his toes. He furrowed his eyebrows.

Pacifica stood before him. She wore a light shawl around her shoulders and had a vaguely expectant look on her face.

"Pacifica?" Shannon asked. "What are you doing out here?"

Pacifica averted her eyes. "Uh, nothing," she murmured, although she had obviously been waiting for him. She opened her mouth to say something, but then closed it again and frowned.

For a girl who usually screamed out what she wanted before considering the consequences, this behavior was highly unusual. Shannon waited.

Pacifica let out a breath. "I was just . . . I was just thinking about what that guy said earlier. Y'know— about how a lot of people would be happy if I died." She spoke calmly and directly, which somehow made it worse. She sighed and gazed up at the sky.

Shannon didn't say anything. He knew Pacifica was past wanting to hear reassuring lies from him.

"If I'd never been born," Pacifica pointed out, "you wouldn't be in this mess."

Shannon took a step in the direction of the camp, shifting slightly to the right to leave room on the path for her. She scuttled up to walk by his side.

"Besides." Pacifica kicked up her own little cloud of dust. "The guy who wants me dead is the king—my real father, right?"

Shannon glanced at her profile as the two strolled toward camp. It took him a moment to search for the right words.

"Maybe," he said quietly, "maybe it's all just . . . some kind of mistake."

"A mistake?"

"Priests are human beings. They're not perfect. Or maybe the others misheard what they said. Maybe even *gods* makes mistakes."

Pacifica smiled weakly. She swallowed.

"Shannon?" she asked in a beseeching, almost childish voice. "Do you, um, believe in me?"

Shannon stopped.

Pacifica turned and looked into his eyes; Shannon's weariness reflected back at him in the intense blue of her gaze.

"Believe in you?" he repeated.

"I mean, is there something about me—anything—that you believe in?"

Shannon sighed. Belief was a difficult concept—despite all the good it symbolized, he also knew it could be used to rationalize selfishness or deny reality. The ghostly image of Sinner cradling his daughter's corpse still haunted Shannon.

"I don't know," he admitted at last. "It's tough to believe in anything."

"Oh." Pacifica paused. She smiled. "Um, thanks. I feel better now."

Shannon furrowed his eyebrows at her again. "That made you feel better?"

"Well, yeah." The girl brushed a strand of hair behind her ear. "I like it when you're honest with me. You didn't lie just to cheer me up."

She cast her eyes downward. "I know I can trust you," she added quietly. "If you end up having to kill me, I'll know there was no other way."

"Don't talk like that," Shannon snapped. Inwardly, however, he was struck by her courage. He knew that faith wasn't an easy thing, particularly when lives were on the line.

"You know," Shannon murmured, "you might make a really good princess."

Pacifica blushed slightly. "You really think so?"

If not for the prophecy, she would have led a royal life. Shannon probably would have never met her.

"Uh, Shannon?" Pacifica asked after a moment.

"What?"

"Please . . . take care of me."

Shannon let out a breath. "Sure," he answered, his words weary but very clear. "That I *can* do."

"I'd like to argue that."

Shannon whipped around, pushing his sister behind him as he did so. He scowled, resentment and frustration etched across his face.

Tactician Christopher Armalight stood in the darkness behind them. Shannon wondered how long the bastard had been standing there.

❧❦❧

A large circle in the pattern of a honeycomb, full of small hexagons, rested in the back of Raquel's mind. It was the data screen she maintained while Asgard was deployed. When someone entered into the detection area, the corresponding hexagonal cell flashed. She could then zoom in on that cell to determine the person's height, weight, stride, and pulse. If she had preprogrammed the data for a specific person, the spell could automatically warn her when that person approached.

But there was a catch. Asgard was a "resident" spell that constantly used some of its sorcerer's mental capacity while activated. Incoming information was still processed (even if the spell-caster was unaware of it) and hence the burden of the spell was usually shared among three or more sorcerers. Any fewer than that and a sorcerer risked diminished mental capacity or even falling unconscious. Raquel had reduced the spell's mental burden by eliminating unnecessary processes and prioritizing the rest, but even using her modified version was only possible because of her tremendous mental capacity.

And she cooked supper while she was at it. Raquel strained slightly as she lifted the iron pot of stew onto the rack over the fire.

"Phew," she breathed, dusting her hands. She shifted her gaze to the small fire and furrowed her brow. The flames weren't nearly as tall as she wanted them to be.

"Maybe I should use a spell," she wondered aloud. "But then I'd have to deactivate Asgard . . ." She threw a bit more kindling on the fire and sighed sadly.

Raquel often resorted to sorcery to solve everyday problems, but that was common for skilled sorcerers—they had to live, eat, and breathe sorcery before it could become second nature.

She had thoroughly memorized basic spells very early in her training, and had learned how to amplify, compress, and otherwise control those spells at will. That had opened the door to the world of complex, powerful spells, most notably military attack spells and special spells. Only rare Grade 1 sorcerers had the level of control necessary for using such advanced magic.

Yet with all her talent, the fire was still tiny. It mocked her with its meager flames.

I won't let it get to me, she thought firmly as she rummaged through the satchel of spice bottles. *I'll just focus on the stew, that's all.* She pulled out a bottle and examined it in the near-darkness.

"Is this the salt?" she asked no one in particular.

Raquel suddenly froze. The Asgard screen popped up in her mind, one of the cells flashing red; someone whose data she'd inputted had entered the detection area. The red cell lay directly next to two other cells that flashed white.

"Shannon," she breathed out. "Pacifica!" She jumped to her feet, letting the satchel and its contents spill to the ground. Bottles rolled in every direction.

She quickly glanced at the mess she'd made. *I'll clean those up later,* she promised as she ran into the darkness.

ॐ

Shannon made the first move.

He took a short step in and lightly crossed his sword with Chris' battleaxe. He wasn't hoping to accomplish anything—it was just a test. With barely a sound, the axe mirrored the movement of Shannon's sword and parried it aside.

He's good, Shannon thought. Most of Shannon's opponents reflexively tried to push back when his weapon struck theirs. A master wouldn't waste energy needlessly resisting an opponent's movements; he would match his own movements to the attack, parrying the weapon and transitioning into a counterattack. It required split-second judgment and an intuition developed through rigorous training and a lot of combat experience.

Shannon knew he couldn't afford to make any mistakes. He stepped back and set his sword in the ready position.

Chris lunged inward, swinging the axe unexpectedly at Shannon's feet. The strange angle of the attack took Shannon by surprise and he was unable to get out of the way; instead, Shannon quickly thrust his sword's tip into the ground to block the axe.

The force of the blow pushed Shannon back a step. *This kid's stronger than me*, he thought as he re-gripped his weapon. As he and Chris circled, sizing each other up, Shannon wondered where the hell Chris stored all his power—the younger warrior was Pacifica's size.

"That's a nice sword," Chris commented, sounding genuinely impressed. "That blow would've broken most blades."

"It's a keepsake of my father's. I couldn't let anyone destroy it that easily." In the back of his mind, however, Shannon knew that a few more swings of that axe could very well snap his heirloom.

"Then this next one's for real." Chris took three steps. The moment he was within striking distance, he swung his weapon with unbelievable speed, parallel to the ground and as high as his head.

Shannon ducked. Without missing a beat, Chris twisted the axe to bring it down diagonally at Shannon, and Shannon barely managed to jerk back and keep his skull intact. While he was off-balance, the axe switched directions again. This time Shannon dodged a fraction too late and the battleaxe left a long cut on his arm.

Chris fought aggressively—always attacking, never hesitating, his axe tirelessly changing directions to make his attacks difficult to block.

Ordinarily an opponent was vulnerable for an instant when his strike was parried, but Chris *never* left himself open. No matter what tactics he tried, Shannon couldn't find an opportunity to attack.

And he was starting to get cut. None of his wounds were serious, but each time he failed to dodge, he was left with another parting gift.

"Shannon!" Pacifica cried after a particularly nasty slice to his forearm. Shannon regained his footing as blood rolled down his wrist.

"Stay back!" Shannon ordered as he dodged another swipe. He let his gaze quickly snap to Pacifica; she still stood well away from the fight, her fists clenched and her eyes wide with fear. "You take one step closer and you will *never* sleep indoors again!"

As the axe came at him once more, Shannon suddenly ducked under the blade and swung at the axe handle. His sword slammed over Chris' hand, locking up under the blade; for the first time since they'd started fighting, the axe remained motionless.

Chris raised his eyebrows. "Not bad," he remarked. "But your technique's a little restrained."

"Shut the hell up," Shannon growled.

"Tell me . . . Shannon, was it? Have you ever killed someone?"

Shannon glared.

"I'll bet you haven't."

"Don't make me tell you to shut up again!"

More than strength, skill, or speed, *that* was the biggest difference between the two warriors.

Shannon had been in many life-and-death battles, but he had never killed any of his opponents. True, it was a testament to his skill that he could defeat an armed enemy without killing him, but his unwillingness to take life still meant a constant, slight hesitation to his technique. Shannon could never fight all-out, for fear of striking that fatal blow. Against a master like Chris, he couldn't afford that hesitation.

The two young men stared at each other over their interlocked weapons.

"I still don't get it," Chris remarked.

"Don't get *what?*"

"Why are you going through all this to protect that girl? What do you gain from it?"

"She's my sister."

"Not a blood sister."

Shannon clenched his teeth. "Why does everyone say that? It doesn't *matter*—in fact, it makes it even more important that I protect her." Pacifica had been abandoned by her real family; if Shannon didn't look after her, who would?

"But what if protecting her means the deaths of thousands of people? She may destroy the world, you know."

Over the past year, Shannon had grown to hate those words. He hated the thought of killing people, hated that he still couldn't be sure he was doing the right thing. But he remembered what Pacifica had said to him:

If you end up having to kill me, I'll know there was no other way.

"Then . . . then *I'll* kill her," Shannon said darkly. "If that's the case, *I'll* kill her. But I won't let anyone else do it. I'm the only one who has the right."

"It isn't a question of rights," Chris said with a wry smile. He twisted the axe in his hands. "This is about strength."

The shaft suddenly folded into thirds. The pressure Shannon had been putting on Chris' weapon turned into forward momentum, propelling his stomach into Chris' raised knee. With a gasp, Shannon fell, landing hard on the ground as his sword clattered beside him.

Chris calmly unfolded his axe to full length again, his ice eyes locked on the floored warrior before him.

"Shannon!" Pacifica screamed.

Dark cloak swishing, Raquel jumped in front of her sister. The sorcerer raised a palm at Chris and rapidly began her incantation.

"O, thou with whom we have entered this pact, lend us thy great power now!"

Chris spun around and prepared to dodge the attack, but there was no need. The landscape failed to explode.

"I guess it didn't work." Chris shrugged. "Too bad. Although maybe it's for the best—using sorcery in close-quarters combat isn't a good idea. You could have missed me and hit your brother."

Chris was right: traditional offensive sorcery was considered most effective against distant targets or as cover fire for attacking troops. But Raquel, of course, had a history of succeeding with unorthodox sorcery techniques.

"Shannon!" Pacifica cried again, panic raising the pitch of her voice. She tried to run to him, but Raquel caught her.

"Let me go!" Pacifica shrieked.

"You'll be killed, Pacifica."

"But Shannon—"

Raquel held Pacifica to her with surprising strength. Pacifica struggled, but couldn't escape Raquel's grip.

"Let me go!" Pacifica screamed. "Raquel, LET ME GO!" With a frantic look in her eyes, Pacifica shouted at Chris as he raised his axe over Shannon.

"Please, wait!" she cried. "*I'm* the one you want! If I die, then no one else will have to, right? So just kill me!"

I want to die as Pacifica Casull, she thought desperately. *If I'm going to die, let me die for the family that's always protected me!*

"D-Don't be stupid," croaked a hoarse voice. Shannon, still on his knees with an arm wrapped around his stomach, glared at her through his dark bangs. "If you keep talking like that, I'll smack you."

"But Shannon—"

"You're *not* going to die." Shannon's tone left no room for discussion. "We'll protect you."

It was what they had sworn to do. It was what gave them strength.

"Repeating spell!" Shannon suddenly yelled. "Activate! Emulator, deploy! Main spell, activate!"

Chris flashed a perplexed look. He wasn't trained as a sorcerer, but he could tell something strange was going on.

Just then, a powerful energy surged from below.

"Dammit!" Chris hissed. He instinctively coiled his body and jumped back, but it was too late.

Twin spirals of white energy erupted from the ground. The explosive torrent shooting skyward threw the boy high into the air, spinning him like a tossed toy. Chris landed hard on his back.

Shannon may have been hopeless when it came to controlling spells, but his enormous mental capacity still allowed him to store them. He had launched Ragnarok, a Grade 1 military attack spell generally used for large-scale military actions.

Sprawled on the ground, Chris fought to breathe. "So," he gasped. "You had . . . a little . . . trick up your sleeve."

Shannon snorted and struggled to his feet. He could see that Chris' clothes were shredded, and that the boy bled from numerous wounds caused by his landing and the impacting heat of Ragnarok—but Chris would clearly live.

Shannon's lack of precision had weakened the spell, and Chris' own last-second dodge had kept him from sustaining lethal injuries.

"You're pretty tough," Shannon muttered as he retrieved his sword. Inwardly, he was relieved that he hadn't killed the boy.

"And you're not a s-sorcerer. So how did you do that?"

"I have the ability, but my control's pretty bad. I had Raquel imprint the spell into my mind so I could launch it like a sorcerer would." Shannon shook his head. "But it's only temporary—I can't launch spells at any time like a real sorcerer."

It had been a risky gamble. An unskilled sorcerer launching Ragnarok could have easily ended in disaster. Shannon had been saving the spell for an emergency like this.

Chris gave a weak grin. "I guess I lost this one," he murmured, looking strangely relieved. His ice-blue eyes rose to Shannon.

"Go ahead. Finish me off."

Shannon shifted the grip on his sword. He knew that if he didn't kill Chris, he'd just have to face the boy again someday. And Shannon wasn't confident that he could defeat Chris again—surprising Chris with sorcery was a trick that would only work once. Killing the boy was the smart thing to do.

Killing. Smart. Two things that Shannon didn't particularly associate with himself.

Shannon let out a breath. "Forget it," he muttered, returning his sword to its scabbard. "It's too much of a hassle."

As Chris looked on in disbelief, Shannon turned and walked to his sisters' welcoming arms.

a Long Journey Begins

"How much farther to the next town?" Pacifica asked as she poked her head out of the coach window.

Shannon shrugged in the driver's seat. "How should I know?"

Raquel was snoring quietly in the coach, seated across from Pacifica. The cloudless blue sky stretched out for what seemed like forever. The road was bathed in warm sunlight, and the contented-looking people who occasionally passed by seemed more attractive than usual. It was an easy day to be in a good mood.

"You don't know?" Pacifica snapped. "Don't you care about anything? You're apathetic—that's what you are! And if there's anything a woman hates in a man, it's apathy! *That's* why you don't have a girlfriend!"

"Whatever," Shannon replied wearily. As usual, that made Pacifica even angrier.

As Pacifica continued to prattle off meaningless insults behind him, Shannon looked up at the sky. The Day of Destiny, when Pacifica would turn sixteen, was less than a year away. That day would mark the end of their journey.

Was the prophecy wrong, or was he?

Shannon looked back to gaze at Pacifica. Noticing his stare, she stopped mid-insult and turned rather pink.

"Wh-What are you looking at?" she demanded.

Shannon shrugged. "Do I need permission to look at you?" he asked. "Maybe I just think you have . . . an interesting face."

"Interesting? You're one to talk!"

We're taking a massive risk, Shannon thought. *We're gonna need a miracle.*

"Besides," Pacifica continued, "you could at least comb your hair or something, Shannon. You're so gross to look at!"

"I'm very sorry, Your Highness."

"Your hair looks like a bird's nest. I wouldn't be surprised if something tried to lay an egg in there." Then, as if suddenly tired from her ranting, Pacifica fell silent.

The sound of the wheels rolling through the ruts in the road settled into peaceful, comforting background noise. Their daily carriage ride was calming, a time when the three siblings could go back to acting like an ordinary family. It served as a bittersweet reminder of the life they had been forced to leave.

Shannon ran his thumb over the reins. So maybe they needed a miracle. Sometimes miracles could happen with faith.

Pacifica looked around distractedly, as if something were on her mind. She leaned toward the dozing Raquel and snapped twice. When Raquel didn't respond, Pacifica pushed herself out of the window and leaned close to Shannon's ear. Shannon continued to watch the road.

"Um, Shannon?" Pacifica whispered shyly.

"Mm?"

She paused. "I . . . I love you."

Shannon, suppressing a yawn, replied, "I know."

An awkward silence followed. A moment later, a red-faced Pacifica threw her arms into the air.

"SHANNON!" she shrieked. "I don't *believe* you! Can't you act happy or embarrassed or something?! You're as apathetic as a corpse!" Her screams filled the warm air.

They still had a long way to go. As Pacifica's tirade continued on behind him, Shannon just sighed.

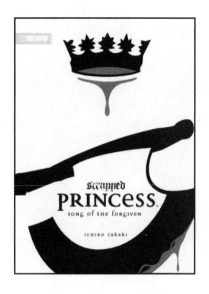

AND COMING SOON:

SONG OF THE FORGIVEN

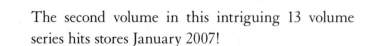

The second volume in this intriguing 13 volume series hits stores January 2007!

scrapped princess volume 2
song of the forgiven

The carriage passed through the gate, leaving the town of Taurus behind.

Pacifica twisted in her seat. She obviously wanted to catch one last glimpse of the town they'd grown so fond of, but Shannon knew it wasn't a good idea. He touched her arm.

"Don't look back," he said, his voice unusually gentle. "It'll just make this harder."

Pacifica turned back in the direction they were headed, her face falling. "You're probably right," she mumbled as she pointed her toes.

"Pacifica."

"Yeah?"

"Get inside the cabin."

An arrow suddenly flew through the air, aimed straight for Pacifica's head; Shannon lunged and managed to catch it before it reached its target. He shoved his sister into the cabin and tossed the arrow away.

"Hey!" Shannon shouted into the scenery that hid the attackers. "I'm having a pretty crappy day. If you're planning to attack me, you'd better be prepared for the worst."

By way of response, arrows soared out of the woods from multiple directions. There were at least four archers in the brush, if not more.

"Wall, defend!" Raquel's voice rang out from the passenger cabin, activating the defensive spell Midgard. Shining geometric patterns surrounded the carriage and horses, deflecting every arrow.

Shannon cracked the whip. "We're going straight through!" he called back.

The barrier disappeared. Without knowing what kind of enemies they faced, Shannon knew that Raquel needed to reserve her magical strength.

Shannon urged the horses onward. He wanted to get as far away from the ambush point as possible—he didn't want to fight assassins in the location they had picked. But before he could get very far, three men with daggers burst from the thicket near the road and leapt for the carriage.

Shannon managed to kick one of the men away, but the other two scrambled onto the carriage. One jumped onto the driver's box, the other on the passenger cabin.

"Dammit!" Shannon cursed. He quickly drew his sword.

In the small driver's box, Shannon couldn't make full use of his sword—a dagger's short range was far more effective. And Raquel couldn't use destructive magic on an enemy who clung to the Casulls' only means of transportation. The enemy had outsmarted Shannon and given themselves a major advantage.

"Who are you?" Shannon hissed. The man wore a black mask over his face, and his clothes had no insignia or marking that Shannon could see.

Instead of answering, the man lunged at him with his dagger. Shannon swiftly brought his sword around to block the blade. Unfortunately, the driver's box wasn't big enough for the maneuver Shannon had in mind; the sword lodged itself in the wall of the passenger cabin with a *thunk*.

"Argh!" Unable to block the dagger, Shannon had no choice but to drop his sword and duck. Despite his efforts, the dagger still sliced through his shoulder.

Shannon's abandoned sword slid out of the wooden cabin wall and clattered off the carriage. Before Shannon knew what was happening, his beloved heirloom was left far behind the speeding coach.

"Impressive," the man muttered. "Few swordsmen are willing to drop a weapon, even if it is a hindrance."

Shannon jammed his hand under the driver's seat and pulled out a short sword he kept there for emergencies. "Shut up," he snapped.

Both men moved at the same moment. The dagger and short sword met with a clash and locked together; both fighters pushed against their weapons in an attempt to overpower the other. Shannon abruptly forced his blade forward and twisted it.

The masked man managed to avoid the blade but lost his balance, and Shannon drove his knee into the man's gut.

For a moment it seemed like the masked man would fall, but he slammed his dagger into the wall of the passenger cabin and used it to anchor himself to the swiftly moving coach. The move jerked the man out of the way of Shannon's short sword, and by the time Shannon had a chance to attack again, the man had already pulled himself onto the roof of the cabin to join his comrade.

Shannon hoped Raquel had something prepared to fight with, but he couldn't think of a spell that would be very effective in such close quarters. Defensive magic could work, but using offensive magic in the cabin would most likely kill everyone.

The men grabbed the edges of the roof and prepared to kick in the glass windows of the carriage from both sides. Shannon was too far away to stop them.

An instant before their feet hit the windows, the glass burst out from the inside. Small steel pellets slammed into the men's ankles and knocked them off-balance. Both men barely managed to catch themselves before they fell.

The rear door of the cabin opened, and Raquel's head and torso appeared over the edge of the roof. She wore strange mechanical contraptions on both her wrists: compatible bows, special high-powered weapons that could launch arrows or steel pellets with great speed. Although her first attack had been through a glass window (and hence had a reduced level of force), even the non-lethal pellets could inflict serious injury at close range.

Raquel smiled. "Just because I'm a sorcerer doesn't mean I always attack with sorcery," she said brightly. The bows on her wrists were still pointed at each of the men.

Good, Shannon thought as he jumped to the roof of the cabin. He knew they had to end the battle quickly, simply because he didn't know how much longer the coach would stay upright without a driver. The stretch of road was mercifully straight, but the carriage could still tip over at any moment.

Under Raquel's watchful gaze, neither man moved. They seemed surprised, but Shannon knew that wouldn't last long—the men were dangerous, too dangerous for either he or Raquel to take on alone. He suddenly realized how much longer the fight could take.

There was only one option left.

"Pacifica!" he shouted. "Take over as driver!"

Pacifica poked her head out of the window. "B-But I've never driven before!" she sputtered.

"Just hold the reins! You're better than nothing!"

Pacifica climbed through the window and tentatively took the reins. Shannon prayed she could handle the task without killing them all.

"So?" Shannon asked, focusing back on the masked men. "What's it gonna be? I'd really like to end this so I can go back for my father's sword."

Shannon's original opponent growled. "I don't recall going easy on you," he snapped, "but I suppose we weren't prepared to take on a trained fighter."

"I don't recall going easy on *you*, but I suppose that was automatic after all the flunkies we've faced." Shannon glanced sideways at Pacifica, then felt the color abruptly drain from his face. His sister had apparently overcome her nervousness and was squealing in delight as she swung the reins wildly.

Don't panic, he told himself in an attempt to calm down. *Just win, then get those reins the hell out of her hands.*

But before Shannon could make his attack, a horse suddenly appeared beside the speeding carriage. The horseman jumped out of the saddle with impressive agility, his gray overcoat spreading out behind him as

197

he soared through the air and landed gracefully beside Pacifica.

He smiled at Shannon. Shannon resisted the urge to scream in frustration.

"Y-You!" was all Shannon managed to strangle out of his vocal chords.

Christopher Armalight winked at a perplexed Pacifica. "Let me do that," he said as he took the reins from Pacifica's unresisting hands.

"Er," she began, confused. "What are you—?"

"For now, we're not enemies." In a display of his peculiar strength, Chris pulled the reins tight. The horses—frightened by the fighting—seemed to regain their senses and eventually slowed the carriage to a stop.

Chris stood up on the seat and spoke in a loud, clear voice without turning to look at the fighters on the roof.

"I have a message from Colonel Sturm," he called. "Code Crimson 0037. He told me you would understand what that meant."

The masked men exchanged a quick glance. In one fluid motion they sheathed their weapons and pulled out thin chains with weights on the end, which they then threw into the trees to the side of the road. Before

Shannon could even make a move, the men swung into the trees and were lost in the forest.

Shannon jumped back into the driver's box. "Hey!" he snapped. "Battleaxe kid! I thought I told you I never wanted to see you again."

"Please call me Chris," the boy said calmly.

Despite Chris' help, Shannon felt a growing urge to throttle the boy. *Haven't I had to beat him enough times already?* he wondered darkly. *And can this day possibly get any worse?*

"You want to tell me what's going on here?" Shannon asked.

"Well, I can't give you the details—they're top secret. But I can tell you that the town is in chaos and that you'd better return."

Pacifica's eyes widened. "What happened to Taurus?!" she demanded.

Chris shrugged. "It looks like the Purgers transformed into a crazy monster," he said evenly. "They're sucking in all sorts of things and growing bigger as we speak."

Shannon opened his mouth to retort the ridiculous statement, but before he could speak a deafening roar pierced the air.

The three Casull siblings whipped toward the sound in shock. Above the familiar buildings of Taurus, giant tentacles swayed violently.